# 31 MA... for Personality Development

One tip a day to better yourself

Abhishek Thakore

PUSTAK MAHAL®
Delhi•Bangalore•Mumbai•Patna•Hyderabad•London

Publishers
Pustak Mahal®, Delhi

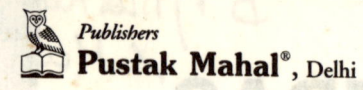

J-3/16, Daryaganj, New Delhi-110002
☎ 23276539, 23272783, 23272784 • *Fax:* 011-23260518
E-mail: info@pustakmahal.com • *Website:* www.pustakmahal.com

London Office
5, Roddell Court, Bath Road, Slough SL3 OQJ, England
E-mail: pustakmahaluk@pustakmahal.com

Sales Centre
10-B, Netaji Subhash Marg, Daryaganj, New Delhi-110002
☎ 23268292, 23268293, 23279900 • *Fax:* 011-23280567
E-mail: rapidexdelhi@indiatimes.com

Branch Offices
Bangalore: ☎ 22234025
E-mail: pmblr@sancharnet.in • pustak@sancharnet.in
Mumbai: ☎ 22010941
E-mail: rapidex@bom5.vsnl.net.in
Patna: ☎ 3294193 • *Telefax:* 0612-2302719
E-mail: rapidexptn@rediffmail.com
Hyderabad: *Telefax:* 040-24737290
E-mail: pustakmahalhyd@yahoo.co.in

© **Pustak Mahal, Delhi**

ISBN 978-81-223-0770-2

Edition : 2007

The Copyright of this book, as well as all matter contained herein (including illustrations) rests with the Publishers. No person shall copy the name of the book, its title design, matter and illustrations in any form and in any language, totally or partially or in any distorted form. Anybody doing so shall face legal action and will be responsible for damages.

Printed at : Unique Colour Carton, Mayapuri, Delhi-110064

Applying the Just for Today Programme

The Just for Today programme is a six-month course in self-development that you can take for yourself.

Requirements:

1. This book, *31 Mantras for Personality Development* 2. A daily journal, 3. A willingness to improve, 4. Commitment to applying the programme.

How to apply this programme:

The basic idea of the Just for Today programme is to make small changes over a sustained period to gain major changes. Decide a time during the day when you can spare 10 minutes – preferably early in the morning.

Time Decided: _____

Daily at this time, read a chapter from the book, randomly or sequentially. But *do not repeat a chapter till all have been done in that particular cycle.*

The book has 31 chapters – one for each day of the month, starting from whenever you begin this book. Don't wait for the start of the month – start now! For the next 31 days, apply a chapter every day, and at the end of that period start the cycle all over again. In six months, you'll have done each exercise six times.

At the end of each day, record your experience in a journal. Just because a particular strategy did not work as well as another, don't skip it the next time! It might click better after some practice. Do not miss the daily journal – just take five minutes before you retire to pen down your thoughts for the day. It will help you face the new day with more enthusiasm.

At the end of the six-month programme, see the kind of changes you've made. I assure you that if you've followed this with the obedience of a child, it will produce the results you want!

RESOLUTION

Starting Date: _____

I, _____ (name) hereby commit myself to the Just for Today programme for a period of six months from this date.

Signature _____

Disclaimer

This book is a compilation of information, techniques and methods used in different therapies, practices and forms of religion, for many generations.

The author, however, makes no claim for effectiveness. The information offered is experience and research-based knowledge. It has to be applied by the reader with his or her judgement and discretion. Because people's lives vary in circumstances and situations the same rules don't apply to everyone. In case of any doubt, please consult professional counsellors or the author himself.

The author, Thakore Centre for Well Being and the publisher of this book are not responsible in any manner for any injury that might occur through following the instructions laid out in this book.

A Few Final Words....

At the end of this journey, I will have shared with you some of the most empowering and profound insights of my life. I need to thank you for giving me an opportunity to share my knowledge.

Apply the principles discussed in this book, and reach for the greatest heights. Hope we cross paths some day. Do come across and share your success story with me. I'd love to know about it. And yes, do stay in touch, and keep learning all the time.

Wishing you the best life has to offer,

Love and Light

Abhishek Thakore
302 A/B Sonakiran
Kanderpada
Dahisar (WEST)
Mumbai – 400 068
E-mail: spiritualentity@softhome.net

Preface

"Day by day, in every way I am getting better and better."

This is a sentence that has virtually transformed my life, sending me on a path of constant and never ending improvement. And in this is captured the very essence, the very nectar of my book, **31 Mantras for Personality Development**.

Welcome to a world where you don't have to change drastically, but little by little! This book is not for the so-called "people on the path" alone. It's for every special person who cares to live a better life. I believe we all at some point of time or the other, had a vision of the kind of life we wanted to live. But somewhere down the line, the vision was lost, as we got more and more caught up in the daily grind of affairs. But hope is still left – and this book is all about making small adjustments, modifications and changes that will yield huge differences.

The power of making small changes constantly is a huge one – much larger than what you could ever imagine. It's very similar to the power of compounding in accounts, which according to Einstein was one of the greatest wonders of the world. Consider this: New York City was sold for $24 ! You might feel that's a very small sum – but wait till you hear this. If the money then received would have been invested at an annual rate of 8%, today that sum would be 27 TRILLION DOLLARS!!!!! That's the power of small changes.

The whole problem is that we are really restless to get results – we want to see changes immediately. Especially when we're putting in time and money into something this important, there is a certain sort of urgency. You want to prove to yourself that the changes are really happening. But be aware of this tendency – not every one of you may get the instant changes that you really want. It will take time.

To illustrate, let me tell you a story. A stonecutter was trying hard to break a huge boulder. So huge in size that most people who passed by nodded their heads in disbelief and discouraged the stonecutter from trying something so gigantic. But patiently, with his small hammer, he kept on hitting repeated blows at the same place on the stone. One whole day passed and nothing happened. The people around him thought that he had gone mad – but the stonecutter was a man on a mission. He was not going to give up all that easily. He continued – the second day, and then the third. Finally in the afternoon of the fourth day, came the magic blow – it split the huge boulder into many chunks.

Was it that single magic blow on the fourth day that split that huge rock, or a total of all the blows from the first one? The answer, is very obvious. And that's what this whole book is also about – applying basic common sense to achieve all that you ever wanted in life. Always remember that the most effective of the knowledge that you'll ever get will also be very simple – the most profound of ideas contain simplicity.

What is the source of this book? Like my previous book, every single insight of this book is completely experiential – you need to experience the joy of applying this. It's common wisdom passed down the ages. Others are tips that I've read in the 250 odd self-development books to date. Yet others are simple suggestions that my friends and mentors have given me, and have worked like magic.

I don't mind admitting that this book is ultimately a compilation. The reason why it was put together was to give you, the reader, a consolidated knowledge bank from which you'd pick up gems that could also be applied instantly.

In order to ensure that all through this book our communication stays as precise as possible, I've used simple language. I have also kept the book as practical as possible, but at the same time remember that doing something by itself is not sufficient – you actually need to know the reason behind what you're doing. So don't just do the In Practice exercises but try to understand the meaning behind each of them.

I consciously chose to put in 31 chapters – one for each day of the month. There was a temptation to put in more, but even these 31 insights, if applied, are powerful enough to transform your life. There is only one condition – you actually need to apply what you will learn.

Use it, or lose it!
Nothing will change in your life if you don't apply all that's outlined here in this book with the faith of a child. I rather recommend you read some great fiction if stories are all that you want to read!

I have one more request for you – don't expect anything from this book! I know that's asking too much, but there is a golden principle regarding this which says: Expectations reduce joy.

Let every chapter, its stories, exercises and results come to you as a surprise, and you'll see the wonderful changes it creates. Don't rely on other's opinions as much as yours – because it's ultimately you who's changing.

At the start of this wonderful journey, let me thank you for giving me an opportunity to share my thoughts with you. I really respect you as a person who is committed to making positive and measurable changes in life – and I'm sure you'll be successful in your effort.

That's a long preface! So I'll end with this prayer:

May every thought in my mind find a perfect word in this book,

And may every word in this book find a perfect thought in your mind!

—**Abhishek Thakore**
Mumbai
14th February 2002

Acknowledgements

As I sit and write *31 Mantras for Personality Development*, a number of people who have been my teachers come to mind, and whom I wish to thank.

First and foremost it will be my parents – my mother who has been an eternal inspiration and made her life a work of art. My father, for being a consultant, a partner, an authority, a friend, a philosopher and a guide – all at the same time.

My sister Akanksha who has always been by my side. Hemang for his encouraging smile, Devang for his suggestions, Shrikant for his enthusiasm, Dhaval for his patience, Kunal for his love and Mirat for his support – I owe my success to this group of friends.

My profound gratitude to Dhaval Bathia, for his guidance during this entire book. Every meeting with him was a lesson of a lifetime. Also to Mr. Bihag Lalaji and family.

To Kanwardeep Singh Arora and Reuben Mistry – two leaders who have brought a positive change in my life through their actions. Also to thank Pankaj Phatarphod – my role model who epitomises perfection in ethics and values. Rajesh, Abhishek and Sudarshan from the Rotaract Movement.

A very special word of thanks to Prof. M K Desai, principal, NM College for his constant support to my activities. His encouragement makes me the super student that I am. Also to the teachers of NM College for setting new standards in teaching, and supporting me always and in all ways.

My thanks to a long list of gurus – Deepak Chopra, James Redfield, Eknath Easwaran, Anthony Robbins, Robert Kiyosaki, Al Ries and Jack Trout, Jack Carnfield and Mark Victor Hansen. Also my revered salutations to spiritual masters – Sri Sri Ravi Shankar for teaching me the Art of Living, Swami Anubhavanandji and Dada JP Vaswani.

All my friends and members of the Blue Ribbon Movement, specially Prateek and Dhruv.

Finally I'd like to thank Mr. Ram Avtar Gupta for his immense trust in me, and Mr. S K Roy and his team at Pustak Mahal, who have put in great efforts to bring this book to you.

—**Abhishek Thakore**

Contents

Preface 5
Just for Today I will Believe It is My Lucky Day 10
Just for Today I will be in Gratitude 14
Just for Today I will Trust My Intuition 18
Just for Today I will be Positive about Everything 22
Just for Today I will Bring Out the Child in Me 26
Just for Today I will be Honest 30
Just for Today I will Do One Good Deed Anonymously 33
Just for Today I will Seek Out One New Experience 36
Just for Today I will Spend Some Time in Solitude 39
Just for Today I will Pray for Someone Else 42
Just for Today I will Treat Everyone
   I Meet as the Most Important Person in the World 44
Just for Today I will Smile Ear to Ear 47
Just for Today I will Take Care of My Body 50
Just for Today I will Spend Time with Nature 53
Just for Today I will Keep an Open Mind 56
Just for Today I will Decide to Remain Happy 58
Just for Today I will Spend Some Time Thinking 61
Just for Today I will Do Some Mental Exercises 64
Just for Today I will Give and be Open to Receiving 67
Just for Today I will Spread the Love 70
Just for Today I will Have Faith in Myself 72
Just for Today I will Act in Congruency 76
Just for Today I will Live in the Present 79
Just for Today I will Listen more than I Speak 82
Just for Today I will be Non-Judgemental 85
Just for Today I will Not Argue at All 88
Just for Today I will Enjoy Little Things 90
Just for Today I will Learn One New Skill 92
Just for Today I will See Things from
   Somebody Else's Point of View 94
Just for Today I will Do the One Thing I had been Postponing 97
Just for Today I will Take Positive Feedback 100

1. Just for Today I Will Believe It is My Lucky Day

Luck is when opportunity meets preparedness. How many of us wish we'd be lucky, in some respect or the other. But at the same time, most of us are hardly prepared to accept that there is an element of hardwork involved too.

Kaun Banega Crorepati is a very popular game show in India. Made on the lines of "Who wants to be a millionaire", the winner of the show stands to win a staggering one crore rupees, which in India is a small fortune. One such episode was being telecast, and I happened to be a "fortunate" viewer.

"What luck! The participant really has the blessings of Goddess Lakshmi. I wish I was there and I'd surely return with a crore," my sister exclaimed.

"Why, did you ever try phoning up the show?" I just asked out of curiosity.

"What's the use? When so many people are trying where do I stand a chance? As it is I'm not all that lucky," she cribbed.

I felt like reminding her of a wonderful quotation: *You will miss 100% of the shots you don't try!*

Luck is a wonderful excuse that mankind has to blame its results on. The fact is nobody but you decide what circumstances you will be in. In the *Bhagavat Gita*, Lord Krishna instructs Arjuna to do the *karma* and not focus his *chitta* on the *karmaphala*. This simply means that you need not worry about the result as long as you have given your best shot. Try your best, and leave the rest on God.

So we have analysed one component of luck – your own efforts are most important. This reminds me of an incident that happened with a prominent golfer. Let's call him John. John and his friend were on the course and John executed a beautiful putt. It flew all over the course and landed right into the hole. It was a perfectly executed shot.

As soon as the ball landed into the hole, the friend exclaimed, "Hey! Lucky man, John! The wind was perfect, and you were perfectly placed for the shot too. I wish I'd get that shot!"

John smiled enigmatically, "Isn't it wonderful? The harder I try, the luckier I get!"

This is the essence of luck – most of it depends on you. But there are certain events totally beyond your control; like a natural disaster or an accident. It can happen to anybody, anytime. Imagine something terrible happening around you. Among the first questions you will hear will be, "Oh God! Why did this have to happen to me? Why am I so unfortunate?"

Remember a golden rule regarding all problems – God matches problems with people. You will never face a problem that you cannot solve, that is the Universal Law. Another important thing is not to refer to problems as problems but as "challenges" or a "situation".

You need to realise that everything that happens to you in a day has some hidden meaning or coincidence behind it. Look at your life so far, and I'm sure you'll find certain events that took place, rather unexpectedly to put you in this situation. The universe sends us messages through these events, and it takes an aware and calm mind to read the clues.

I was told that Dr. Deepak Chopra – my guru and the man who popularised alternative therapies in the States – narrates a very interesting story on how he entered the world of holistic medicine. During one of his flights he came across a book on Ayurveda. After a while, he found the person sitting next to him talking about alternative medicine. Finally, on alighting at the airport he found that a convention of Ayurveda had been organised! This series of coincidences was what Dr. Chopra decided to follow, only to evolve from a medical practitioner to the New Age guru that he is today.

By believing that today is your lucky day, you spend the day in positive anticipation. You need to hope for the best, yet be prepared for the worst. Generally, though, what happens in a day is what you expect. People too behave the way they are expected to.

At the same time, even if something terrible happens to you, remember that today is your lucky day, and this event has to have a higher meaning. It is part of a larger picture. You need to ask yourself, "Where does this lead me to?" or "What can I learn from this?"

Some of the major decisions in my life have come during times of unpleasant incidents, when life took a drastic step to make me realise something. And one needs to feel lucky that one could decipher what was being implied.

Finally, you need to be grateful for all the good things that happen to you. There are millions of people less fortunate around you, who don't have basic things that we take for granted, like food, shelter or even education. There are thousands fighting for freedom, and billions below the poverty line. Among the rich too, different diseases and problems are prevalent. Compared to them, you're far better off. Doesn't that make you feel incredibly lucky?

IN PRACTICE

1. Realise that your circumstances are a result of your past decisions and not fate. Make decisions consciously from now on.
2. Try to find the deeper meaning behind each event, each person that you meet today.
3. Be aware and grateful for the wonderful gifts life has given you. At the same time be open to better things and events happening.
4. Make a list of the events that seem unique in your life, and find the deeper meaning to them. Maintain a journal like this:

Date :

Event :

_____

_____

Deeper Meaning :

_____

_____

5. Value analysis

Make a list of things that you value the most in life – things like happiness, security, freedom, learning etc. This will be a guide for you to make choices. List 10 of your values. To find a value, ask yourself, "What is important to me?"

My Values :

_____

_____

_____

_____

Now see if they are in order, i.e. compare each value with the other to find if it is actually the order, starting from importance.

Happy Lucky Day!

2. Just for Today I Will be in Gratitude

We all want to be BIG – to grow and evolve. To realise our dreams and achieve our goals. But do you know the easiest way to be BIG?

Be In Gratitude

This might seem an innocent sentence at a glance – but don't get misled by it! It indeed has the power to transform the entire outlook of life. It is all about changing the way you look at life and people in general. It is a great way – the way of gratitude.

Let's imagine a hypothetical situation – that you want the town to be painted red. If you want the town to be painted red, there are two ways to go about it. First, you can hire a huge army of workers, and send them all around with red paint and get the job done. Obviously, this is not possible, unless you're as rich as Bill Gates and as influential too. And not to mention that every single resident of the town will be cursing you for your choice of colour!

But there is a shortcut – a cheat code. The second way is to simply wear red-coloured glasses! Even though nothing may be red, the glasses will filter everything so much so that it will appear red to you. This reminds me of a popular saying, *You can't carpet the earth, but you can wear a pair of footwear.*

Gratitude is the glass that you'll need to look at the world through. I see many young people around me today, who have a burning desire to rebel and to change this world. If you hear the lyrics of some popular rock songs, you'll find the spirit of rebellion echoing in them. But the question is, why try and change the world? The world, or for that matter the entire universe, is the way it should be at this moment.

Struggling against things is like banging your head against a mountain. There is always a way around it. Though it is neither easy nor practical to make the entire world be the way you want it to be, it is always possible to work with your own outlook.

What exactly is being in gratitude all about? It's about simply being thankful for things that you have in life. Once you try to imagine, you will realise the infinity of things that you have to feel grateful about. There is a song in Hindi that when translated means, "There is such a lot of sorrow in this world, and my sorrow is so less. When I saw the grief of the people around me, I forgot my own..."

If you look at your life, you will realise that there are so many things you can be thankful for. While reading this book, you need to be thankful to all your teachers who taught you to read. Ask an illiterate the value of education and you'll know how important your skill is. Less than half this world is literate, so that already puts you in the upper half! What about the publishers of this book? They are the ones who took all the pains to get this book into your hands, but for which we wouldn't have had a chance for an intimate dialogue like this. The printer, the people who made the paper, the light under which you're reading this book... the list can go on and on.

A very interesting thing about life is that you realise the value of a thing only when it is not there. I remember the morning I woke up to find my washbasin clogged. I was so used to the basin that I could neither brush, nor shave properly. And the frustration lasted the entire day. Little did I know before that fateful day that a mere washbasin is so important to me in life! Look at things around you – you'll realise their value only in their absence.

This is more true for people. I've seen people being ignored and cursed during their lifetimes. But the day they die, every single person feels sorry. The fact is that we tend to take all good things in life for granted. We take all our relationships for granted too.

And gratitude makes you aware of this, and realise the importance of small things.

You need to be grateful for every single thing that helps you in life. One really humbling experience is to express gratitude to your footwear. Sounds ridiculous? You have never done it before? Then stop reading right now. Take a minute to go to your footwear and tell it mentally that you are grateful to it for the way it protects your feet. Tell your footwear that you value it. Do it now.

How did it feel? You will realise the importance of this exercise the next time you wear your footwear. I took to the practice of expressing gratitude to my shoes. One fine morning, my left shoe began to bite! I mentally requested the shoe to become comfortable and thanked it once again for being comfortable all this while. Trivial though it may sound, within the next few steps the shoe actually stopped biting. Cynics might scoff calling this a placebo effect, but for me it was a miraculous result, and that's all that counts.

What about people? When was the last time you expressed to someone you love that you do? I'm sure it was a long time ago! So what are you waiting for? At times we tend to feel that such things are assumed, but assumptions can be made both ways. Also, it feels better when such things are expressed. Learn to care for people and be grateful for what they've given you. Your parents have given you life, your teachers, knowledge. Even your enemies have given you a chance to improve on something – so be grateful to every single person you know of. Don't leave yourself out!

Similarly you can be grateful for any event in your life. You can be thankful because the worst could have happened. And there will always be people who are in more challenging circumstances than you. God hasn't given all problems to you alone. So thank everyone, and grow – grow to become BIG... to Be In Gratitude.

Ultimately, the only thing I say is you can either be grateful or a great fool. Take your pick!

IN PRACTICE

1. Do the self-gratitude exercise. Sit in a calm, quiet place. Starting from your hair to the toes, express gratitude to each and every part of your body for the vital role played by them. Give yourself a motherly touch too.
2. Recollect the most unpleasant incident of your life, and find ten reasons to be grateful that it happened.
3. Express gratitude to loved ones. It need not be in words – it can be through actions too.
4. Make a list of at least 50 things you should be grateful for. Express gratitude to each, mentally.
5. Whenever something happens, express gratitude that it happened. You will thus be able to change your viewpoint to it.
6. Learn to thank the abstract forces of nature for the weather, including simple gifts like sunshine and flowers!

Finally, let me start by expressing gratitude to you for having read, and hopefully applied this chapter. You have also given me an opportunity to share my knowledge.

Thank you.

Learning Story : Five Cents

When an ice-cream sundae cost much less, a boy entered a coffee shop and sat at a table. A waitress put a glass of water in front of him. "How much is an ice-cream sundae?"

"Fifty cents," replied the waitress.

The little boy pulled his hand out of his pocket and studied a number of coins in it. "How much is a dish of plain ice-cream?" he inquired.

Some people were now waiting for a table, and the waitress was impatient. "Thirty-five cents," she said angrily.

The little boy again counted the coins. "I'll have the plain ice-cream."

The waitress brought the ice-cream and walked away. The boy finished, paid the cashier, and departed. When the waitress came back, she swallowed hard at what she saw. There, placed neatly beside the empty dish, were two nickels and five pennies—her tip.

Gratitude List

Now spend a few moments making a gratitude list – a list of things that you're really thankful for in your life.

Ideal target – 100.   Minimum target – 50.

Till you don't reach the target, just keep asking yourself, "What am I grateful for?"

Start right away!

My Gratitude List

_____
_____ ◆◆

3. Just for Today I Will Trust My Intuition

Those were the days of our college festival, when one fine evening I thought of a naughty prank. One of my friends had been meditating for five years or so, and meditation, if practiced well, makes you spiritually evolved. What you want happens, and your gut feeling becomes almost accurate.

So I decided to test my friend – and hid one of his books in the locker. When he came looking for it, I told him that I had hidden his book in one of the 24-odd lockers. He had to find out which one. I made a big show out of it, and caught the attention of everyone around. But my friend was calm all the while and, to cut a long story short, the first locker he opened had the book!

Sounds miraculous to you? Not for him, because he was one of those people who had consciously developed his sixth sense or intuition. That was not the only incident that I shared with him. In the course of our friendship, many times we encountered situations where a spontaneous decision was required. And my friend's decision, though not in consonance with the majority, would turn out to be correct in the end.

A cynic might scoff at this, but I am a strong believer in intuition. What is this intuition, you may ask. Intuition can simply be described as the gut feeling about a certain event or person. You feel that something will happen in a certain way, and it does happen so.

Look back at your life. You too will surely recall times when you felt a certain way about something and that turned out to be correct. Especially when with people closest to you, this happens often. You hear something and realise that this was exactly the same thing you wanted to say. Or sometimes, you and another person begin humming the same song together. Hasn't it happened?

Trivial though it may sound, intuition is a great tool to guide you in life. Science is now gradually discovering the morphogenetic field – a pool of all thoughts of mankind accessible to all of us. Intuition is merely a message from this field, or even your surroundings.

The over-rational approach of our day-to-day life has surely taken us far away from the magical, mystical world. And that is why most of these messages are ignored and dismissed as random thoughts. How many of us make the mistake of not listening to our intuition, but later realising that we should have?

Just for today, you will decide not to doubt your intuition. If you feel like doing something you think will help or be worthwhile, do it. If you get a message about someone, tell him or her. Who knows, you might end up saving a life.

At this point, let me make a distinction. There is a very thin line between a thought and an intuition. A thought is very mental in nature. It is just in the mind. An intuition, on the other hand, generally has a bodily response attached to it. When you get an intuition, your heart too feels it. Many of us also experience a sense of thrill when such a thought strikes.

So remember that most of your initial attempts will be more of thoughts than intuitions. Developing intuition was a really challenging process for me, in the sense that initially I would often end up becoming the laughing stock of people around me. Gradually though, a developed intuition gave me untold rewards.

How do you develop intuition? It is simply by following your hunch or gut feeling. The moment you feel something, at least tell it to someone. Be detached thereafter, and even if it turns out to be correct, don't make a big noise about it. What if it is wrong? Never mind, remember: try and try till you succeed.

Developing intuition can be supplemented by having a healthy diet comprising fresh food, raw vegetables and fruits. Also practise meditation, because it will get you closer to the field of intuition. Any form of meditation such as TM (transcendental meditation), chanting a mantra, Vipassana, preksha dhyana and the like are useful.

People who have a clean heart and conscience are generally blessed with better intuition. So harbour no ill feelings against anyone. Ultimately, this magical facility will develop the more it is used and trusted. So use it – or you lose it!

In a broader sense, intuition also means your feelings. Whenever you have a decision to make, listen to your heart as well – if you feel comfortable with a certain decision, only then go ahead with it. Nothing will succeed if you have lurking doubts about its failure. This makes intuition a great tool for decision making too.

Finally, there are a lot of games you can play to improve intuition. Most of them are games of chance, a few of which I have outlined in the In Practice section of this chapter. Remember, developing intuition is a long process that you are starting today. But if it were easy, would it be worth developing at all?

IN PRACTICE

1. Games of intuition
   You can start with coins – guessing which side the coin will land. Anything over 50% can be counted as your intuition. Then move on to dice and card suits, card numbers and then the actual cards themselves. You will eventually be able to gain more and more accuracy.
2. When you get a hunch, tell someone close to you about it or write it down. Make sure you keep a track of how much of it came true.
3. Meditate regularly.
4. The next time you make a decision, also consult your heart.
5. Just for today, dare to follow your gut feeling. Be sure to stay detached to the result though!

Heart process

Close your eyes

Start breathing deeply, and relax every single part of your body.

If there is discomfort in any part, mentally request it to relax.

Focus attention on your breathing for some time.

Now feel your heart fill with love.

Let the love expand into your entire body – give love to your entire body.

Feel yourself swimming in a river of love – and let that love expand to the room, your house, locality, city, state, country and the whole earth.

Finally feel the love from your heart fill up the entire universe – that makes everyone happy and peaceful.

Now place your right hand on your heart and shift attention to your heart – it has been beating without rest ever since you were born, at your service all the time. Thank it mentally, and wait for your heart or inner voice to respond.

At this stage you can ask anything you want from your heart – any question or doubt. The heart is holistic – so never discount what comes from the heart.

When you've finished asking all that was, spend some time with your eyes closed becoming aware of your surroundings. Finally when you feel relaxed, open your eyes with a broad smile on your face.

◆◆

4. Just for Today I Will be Positive About Everything

We are made to believe that this world is composed of two forces – the good and the bad – or more appropriately, the positive and the negative.

The positives are things and events that we tend to feel good about, whereas the negatives are the painful ones. You never know what will come up – and just like everyone else, you too most probably fear the presence of the negative in your life. You don't want the pain that's associated with everything that's negative. You just want the positive.

But who decides what comes to you? Is it fate? Is it your past life karmas? Or is it God randomly deciding to give you doses of pain and pleasure? If you ask me, I'll reply –it's you! Yes, you decide whether what comes to you is positive or negative.

A classic example of the optimist-pessimist battle is the half-glass story. An optimist calls the glass half full whereas the pessimist calls it half empty. This difference shows that both react differently to the same situations. In essence, YOU DON'T HAVE ANY CONTROL OVER THE SITUATIONS YOU FACE. BUT YOU HAVE COMPLETE CONTROL OVER YOUR REACTION TO THE SITUATION.

No one can actually choose or even predict the trend of events that life throws up. But what you have control over is your reaction. That is the choice that you're making. You must make it consciously. This is the time to choose the positive.

The negative has a strange magical power of influence imparted to it. Put a rotten potato in a basket of completely good ones, and soon the rot spreads. Somehow, nature has given a challenging battle to man. If your loved one gets late, you imagine hundreds of things that could have happened to him or her. Most of them will not be positive. Of the thousands of thoughts we have every day, around one percent are positive. Those are the odds we are up against!

At this point, let me introduce the 9:1 principle: *For every event that happens and has one negative effect, there are nine positive ones.*

The only problem with us is that we seldom look at the nine positives – we just devote all our energy and attention to the one irritating negative point. After consuming the energy, this negative grows to overshadow our mind – till we are almost driven to believe that the event was truly a negative one.

Trust me, even the most negative events of life will have a positive side to it – it only requires the power of perception to see it. Maybe the illness of a loved one brought you closer to him. Or the loss of some possession made you realise its value and be more careful about it in the future. That's the magic of the right perspective!

Positive Mental Attitude is something that Pays More Always. I remember the case of one of my friends, whose father fell seriously ill. He was totally shattered since cancer was detected. "Life is so unfair!" he said. He lost his father within two months. This event was the most painful one in his life.

However, when he attended my workshop, I insisted he apply the 9:1 rule to this event too. Initially, he was extremely sceptical, but eventually did so. He then realised that the illness had made him come much closer to his father. He never used to spend time with his family, but the illness forced him do so. He began to care for his mother more than before. He learned to value people when they were alive. And he began to donate to the Cancer Aid Association. So many positive transformations!

A lot of people believe that the optimist is not a realist. People who think positive deny problems. This is definitely not the case. True positive thinking rests on the mantra:

Hope for the best
Prepare for the worst

Positive thinkers anticipate positive things happening. However, they know that things can go wrong. But because they focus on the positive, they are able to handle such situations much better. They have the mental peace and attitude to tackle problems rather than crib about them.

One of the major temptations of thinking negative is that if you've done so, when things go right, it gives you a pleasant surprise. What you must realise, though, is that you see what you look for. More often than not, the universe responds to your expectations. This is something that's better experienced than read about. When you become positive, the journey becomes very enjoyable and full of positive anticipation. As for the destination, you are in a better position to reach there too.

What happens when you fail in spite of thinking positive? Remember, thinking positively is not an insurance against things going wrong. Good old Murphy's Law still holds good! But when a positive thinker fails, instead of feeling defeated, he simply asks himself, "What can I learn from this?" For the positive thinker, there are no failures – only learning experiences. Isn't that a great way to become a perennial winner?

IN PRACTICE

1. Applying the 9:1 rule
   Apply this new rule today to at least one painful incident that happened to you in the past – this will help you heal the incident and gain perspective.
2. Expect the people you meet to be on their best behaviour. Surprisingly, you'll observe that they respond to your expectations.
3. If things don't turn out to be the way you want them to, don't lose patience. Look for the positive in them too.
4. Watch your thoughts – the moment you find yourself thinking negative, tell yourself "STOP!" This will prevent the mind from going into a negative groove.
5. Read the chapter on detachment – "Just for today I will remain detached." Positive thinking works best with detachment.
6. Past event analysis.
   Pick up any event of the past that has always bothered you
   Describe it in brief here.

_____
_____
_____
_____

Now try and look at the positive side to it – how bad could things have been worse and what you learnt from it. This will require an open and honest mind. Make a list of nine such reasons. You may not get all nine at the first go, but do keep asking – and sooner or later it shall be revealed!

_____
_____
_____
_____

◆ ◆

5. Just for Today I Will Bring Out the Child in Me

A survey across the world asking people about the "best days of their life" would give a unanimous opinion – childhood! The beautiful memories of childhood are cherished by each one of us – times when we were so innocent and pure, so carefree, so very blissful. Doesn't it make you nostalgic when you see children romping around?

Where does childhood vanish? As we grow, expectations of our peers and society at large increase. Everyone expects you to behave in a "mature" fashion. Surprisingly, this behaviour takes away the joys of being a child. Also, as you grow, you come to know of this "Big Bad World", which makes you jaded. It makes you a realist, and buries the child in you deep within.

But the child is there. Have you seen the way adults behave at amusement parks when they sit in rides? They are excited, relaxed, enthusiastic... just like children. Trust me – there is a child within each one of us, you and me included. A child that is innocent and doesn't want to harm anyone on purpose. A child that knows that there is someone to care for him, and so he need not worry. A child that is loved and loves without any prejudice. A child that loves to play and is playful!

So bring out that child in you today. No, I'm not asking you to speak with a lisp, fight over petty things or be childish. Be childlike. Take in the more beautiful aspects of being a child. For today, feel carefree. Be aware that God is there to take care of your needs. Don't be bothered by anything – stock markets, petrol prices or neighbours. Dare to be free of worry, with a secured feeling that things are the way they are supposed to be.

Most of us stop playing games when we grow up. So today, dig up your favourite board game and play it with friends. Or download your favourite video game from the Net and just play till you want. You may even join in some outdoor sport, but remember not to strain yourself, or you'll be up with a body ache!

As a child, you will notice we were very spontaneous. We reacted and responded to stimuli instantly. If there's a song that you love you'd sing along, without bothering how nice or rough your voice was. If there was a jingle you loved, you'd get up and start dancing. Try practicing this spontaneity too. Also remember, not to hide your reactions. A child doesn't wear a social mask. But it gradually gets trained to wear one. It is nothing but a set of reactions that are expected. So as a child, for today you will be spontaneous.

The world doesn't look at you the way the people closest to you do. So also, do not act childishly before others – just make sure people don't see you acting foolish and make a big deal out of it. The living example of this is my mother. To the world she is a lady who will laugh only when necessary, very poised and calm. But at times, at home, she becomes a child – literally! She dances and sings and what not! And all of us have a great time in the process. Try it and you'll see the positive energy flow out.

Seeing children at play is an act that has kept me absorbed for long hours. Playing with children is fun, for you can become a child again. I've seen so many adults who enjoy doing this, for that's the only excuse they have to become children again. That's how they can recite nursery rhymes and go kootchie-coo. In all other situations, the social mask prevents them from doing such things.

So if you feel hesitant about being the child all by yourself, be so with some child – that is socially acceptable! And when the child smiles back at you, you'll see the joy that it fills you up with. Any wonder why an increasing number of ads are using children? To emotionally blackmail us!

It's basically all about enjoying what you do and doing what you enjoy. So if you really enjoy being a child, why not be one? You can call all the children to your place and have a bash with them too. You'll be the most famous uncle in the locality, and the children will flock around you too!

The truth of the matter is that you are still a child deep within, but you aren't allowed to be one. No problems! You can still do these things and be a child again! One more thing that I love about children is the fact that they are so humble and willing to learn. Ever heard of an egoistic child? No way! So for today, you will also leave behind your ego and become a learner. Listening to others, like good kids do!

Most of us love children – why? Because children are so special. They're innocent and natural. They love others without any prejudice – that's what a child can do that we cannot. So as a child for the day, love everyone without any hesitation. Remember, everyone is waiting to get love – and you can start out by being the giver.

At the end of the day, recollect your day's experiences. You'll see that spending even an hour as a child was beneficial – and fills you with positivity. So don't wait – reverse your age right away!

IN PRACTICE

1. Pre-plan the day/time when you'll bring out the child.
2. Plan some games or activities that you had enjoyed in the past but never found time to go back to.
3. One of the best ways to bring out the child from within is to play along with children – you'll be surprised to see the wonderful transformation.
4. For the moment, be spontaneous. Don't hesitate in talking your mind out. Also be obedient to everyone – just like a child.
5. This becomes even more enjoyable when you do it in a group – the kids group. Just make sure you do it in privacy.
6. Singing and dancing like children can be a lot of fun too. My personal favourite is the birdie dance – anyone can dance it without prior knowledge of dancing.

Further Reading :

MY CHILDHOOD
Whenever I see a child, I remember my childhood,
Everything was so beautiful. Everything was so good!
My mind was free of tensions. My mind was free of worry,
Sorrow and Grief were miles away, and so were haste and hurry!
When I see a child, so many things it does remind,
I remember the innocent face and the burden free mind,
As a child I was so timid. As a child I was so meek,
I used to be friends with joy, the same joy that today I seek.
As a child many things, I could never understand,
But on every step of my life, I had a helping hand,
Today when I have grown up, I feel so forlorn,
In this mean and bad world I am alone,
It is indeed a woeful tale. It is indeed an unwanted boon,
That we learn bad ways so fast, and childhood passes away so soon.
Is this the curse of growth? Has time given us this bane??
That childhood goes down the memory lane?
But even today the thought of being a child,
Drowns me in joy and drives me wild!!!

—**Abhishek Thakore**
◆ ◆

6. Just for Today I Will be Honest

Pinnochio was in trouble! He was a compulsive liar. But now he was in a situation where whenever he'd lie, his nose would grow. How I wish this would be true in real life too! If this would be the case, how long would your nose be?

A childhood sermon we've heard over and over is "Honesty is the best policy". I read the latest version of this at a station, where a signboard proclaimed: "Honesty is the best policy... with a little bit of common sense!"

Truth is very powerful. And it can't be hidden for long. Truth is what a simple man with a loincloth used to shake the foundations of a worldwide empire. Yes, I'm talking about the Mahatma – who used satyagraha successfully to topple the British Government.

Most of us think that telling lies is a great way to escape problems. We like to believe that the person we are lying to can't make out. Nothing can be further from the truth. People closest to you will always be able to make out if you're lying or not. As for strangers, they'll eventually discover that you fib. With the result that people will begin to discount what you say.

There are many such people around us who talk a lot of hot air – they are never taken at face value. Remember, empty vessels make more noise. In a particular organisation where I'd worked, whatever the marketing department said was always divided by two! They had earned the dubious reputation of exaggerating the smallest of facts. In plain words, they were used to lying.

But more important than being honest with others is being honest with yourself. Most of us can't grasp this concept. If you observe yourself, you'll notice you are constantly talking to yourself – what you say at this time is really important. If you've done something that's wrong, it is most difficult to admit it – but that's exactly what you've got to do. If it's a failure, you can get away by blaming someone or something else for it. Some optimists even label it a success and feel happy about it. But that's not the way it works! It is important that you accept your shortcomings first. Only then can you improve on them.

Shakespeare said: "To thine own self be true" – which means not denying problems but accepting them and acting on the solutions available.

Honesty has broader implications too. Being honest also implies that you do your duty honestly. If you're a student your primary duty is to study – you need to realise that if you're not doing that it's a way of being dishonest. You need to do your own job to the best of your abilities. As it's said, even if someone is a sweeper, let him be the best sweeper in the world, and he'll be a master!

What are the payoffs of honesty? The single biggest payoff is a clear conscience. When you look at yourself in the mirror, you'll be proud to see a person of integrity. You will be happy about the fact that you've been strong enough to stick to your principles. A clean conscience is the best sleeping pill you can ever have.

Look at the immense trust you'll get from people. In a world filled with people who're ready to sacrifice values and principles at the slightest temptation, someone who can actually stand by the truth is someone very valued. You build a big trust fund. When people trust you, they will be more open to you. They will be attracted to you and help you when you're in need.

In life there are so many situations that give us an opportunity to be honest. There are times when someone charges you less, or returns you some extra change. At such a time, by being dishonest, you may gain a few rupees – but your honesty may save someone's job. And when more and more people start being honest, you too will find yourself on the receiving end. Whatever you give comes back to you – so remember that when you're cheating and lying, you're ensuring that you too will be cheated and lied to.

I can visualise you thinking, 'All this is fine, but being 100% honest is just not possible in this world.' Remember, there's a saying: *Satyamvada Priyamvada* – if you have to speak a lie that benefits someone, it's better than a truth that hurts. The responsibility is yours – choose to use your ability to lie as wisely as possible.

It may be very tempting to lie and get away from the situation – but having guts to tell the truth pays in the long run. You can never hide something forever – it WILL always come to light. So choose the option that pays in the long run – honesty!

IN PRACTICE

1. Whenever you realise that you're not doing your duty, be aware and alert – and start again.
2. There will be opportunities that tempt you to be dishonest – be strong enough to refuse them.
3. Pray to God for strength to stick to your principles.
4. Set up a reward-punishment system for yourself – whenever you find yourself telling lies, punish yourself and reward yourself when you stick to the right side. The rewards and punishments can be anything material or non-material.
5. Every time you observe this day track your progress – how well you did. You will realise that with enough practice you'll be able to stick to it longer.

Recording your progress

Date :   Day :

Event	Analysis

Analysis will include the reasons and effects of the event.

Make sure you keep this confidential, or you'll be the most famous liar around!

◆◆

7. Just for Today I Will Do One Good Deed Anonymously

Treat others as you would like to be treated. When I look around at the world, I'm simply overwhelmed by the number of things that can be improved. There are so many out there who need support, who need help. If you too were observant, you'd realise the immense scope of helping around.

As humans, we've made many questionable choices – which have brought us to this stage. If UN statistics are to be believed, one per cent of the global war funding can be used to feed every living person on the planet. And according to economist John Fuller, there is enough wealth in the world for each of its six billion people to be millionaires! What a thought!

The very fact that you're reading this book, and I assume you have access to basic necessities, puts you in the upper half of the world population. We might crib at our dinner table, and never pause to think about African countries that are at war against each other over basic issues for decades. We may complain when our parents don't allow us something – without bothering to think of countries still struggling for freedom.

If you look for comparisons around the world, you'll realise how absolutely fortunate you are. You are definitely among the blessed – so don't you feel you must share a part of this good fortune with others? You must understand that when you start to do this, you will be giving to people who need more than you – and create value in the world.

Your good deed can be for just about anyone around you. It must bring value to the life of the person you're making it to. It should be a deed – an action that has a consequence. Look around you, and you'll find at least one good thing you can do to help people close to you.

The most important condition, however is that it must be done anonymously. Why? When you do a good deed, your internal response is to grab credit for it. But when you do the deed anonymously, your ego isn't unnecessarily boosted. If you've done something good, only you need to know. That's enough. You don't need to seek the approval of the entire world for your actions.

It is almost magical – the beauty of doing something secretly will make you realise that true greatness is unsung. And because it is anonymous, the receiver also enjoys it more. The person who receives it may not even realise that it's something new or extra. Sometimes, the person may take it as an act of God.

God is the greatest giver. He has given us this world, this life. Yet, he's never ever told you: "Look, I've given you this and that. Now you must do so and so and behave in this way." It's without expectations – just the way it must be. So when you give, you must realise that God is working through you, secretly. He is making you a channel. Doing this anonymous deed will bring out the best of your hidden qualities. It will be the noblest form of you.

I knew my sister is really interested in animal rights. So one day when I browsed the PETA site, I registered. But I used her name. Since then, she keeps receiving posters and newsletters. Surprisingly, she's never paused to think how she's receiving this, or why it comes in her name only. And although I've been tempted, I've never told her. I've let that be the anonymous good deed.

Your good deed could be anything. It could be an anonymous letter to somebody, telling him or her all the good things about him/her. It could be a small gift that you just slip into their cupboard. Be sure not to get caught – you'll learn with practice! You can do or give almost anything – the possibilities are limitless.

If you want, keep track of all the anonymous good deeds you've done. There will be times when you'll feel particularly down and low – just read the list and it'll make you feel better! Imagine the time on your deathbed – what will you value more? Will it be all your possessions, your houses and cars? Or will it be such deeds? The answer should be obvious.

IN PRACTICE

1. The practice of today's principle begins with an awareness of how fortunate you are. Be aware of the reasons you need to be grateful for.
2. Make a list of ten reasons why it's great to be born in your present circumstances. It could be about your country or your life situation – just about anything.
3. Think of the people around you – both known and strangers. What would they appreciate as a good deed? In fact, you can ask yourself the same question and make a list of such things.
4. Do the actual thing – there might be some resistance, but remember there's nothing to lose. No one is going to fight with you for being so nice! So go ahead, and do it.
5. Inspire others around to do this too – you'll spread this beautiful thing to many others, and that itself is a great deed.

List of possible activities
- Donating something in cash or kind to charity.
- Write a letter as an anonymous admirer.
- Do something for somebody that you've been procrastinating about.
- Now add your own to this list.

◆◆

8. Just for Today I Will Seek Out One New Experience

As soon as you enter a party, you're most likely to look for someone you know. When you meet someone else, you try and find what's similar between you two. When you know the way things are likely to turn out, you feel safe. You are more secure in your home than you'd ever be in some foreign country.

If you look at the basic conditioning of the mind, you'll realise that it is hell-bent on seeking one thing – familiarity. Whatever is familiar and known naturally appears to be more enchanting to the onlooker. Millions of rupees are spent in advertising – only to increase familiarity with the products. Your mind naturally seems to love the familiarity.

However, if you look back on your life, you'll discover an interesting truth. Whenever you've grown or learnt, it has been from something new, something untried. When you took your first step as a baby, you were full of uncertainty – but gradually, even though you fell, you soon learned to walk proficiently.

Your life can simply be judged by the new experiences that you've had. Take the case of Mr. Aay who has a set routine for six days a week throughout the year. But Mr. Bee lives each day differently. If you consider his experiences, you'll see that Mr. Bee has lived much more. Read the article at the end of this chapter to gain a clear insight into what is being talked about.

When you reach out for the new, you are growing. This itself should be the greatest security for yourself when you actually go "out there". Your mind will definitely resist the idea of the new – and want you to go back to the old things. But it's your resolve that must win. After all, you've got nothing to lose! All you have to do is try something that's untried.

A principle that I've developed is particularly helpful – it's called Action Now. There are many times in life when you're faced with a challenging choice – with regard to the course of action you must pursue. Usually, the two conflicting options will be the new and the old – the tried and the untried. Your primary response will be to delay the action as long as possible – and stay immobilised.

At such a time, remember the first word – Action. It means that you need to act. You must choose action over inaction.

But the mere choice of action is of no use if it's postponed. Action must happen NOW – immediately. Let's look at a real life example for better understanding. When I used to travel by bus, I met smiling people who'd cheerfully beam back at me. I always wanted to talk to them, but somehow, I always convinced myself not to. I choose inaction. That was till I got the mantra – now I jump in and talk. Many times, I've received a really sad response, but that does not scare me. Because there have been times when I have discovered some really wonderful people.

Your new experience for the day can be anything – you may eat something that you've never tasted. You may explore a place you've never been to. Or you may meet and talk to someone new. You can try mastering a new skill too. It's very easy, once you have the hang of it. But remember, it must be new.

With the way our lives go, in a routine we soon start becoming uncomfortable with anything that's new. If you look at someone old, you'll see how much "into" their routines they are! If there is a minor disturbance, they feel irked. When something new is happening you are actually growing – adding to the memories that will be so important to you when you're old. So begin today, and start seeking new experiences.

Extra Reading

More life per life!
Yeh dil maange more!
When you look back at the year gone by, how well did you live it? Which wonderful memories linger on – the day you fooled the peon and entered college, your greatest blunder of the year and the days you were most naughty? How can someone ever remember the "normal" days – when everything was just the same! But dear friend, do ask yourself whether you lived 365 different days or the same day 365 times in the year gone by?

Life is a wonderful gift, but it is different experiences that ultimately constitute life. You go through different events, which ultimately get framed in your mind as beautiful memories. So it's not the years in your life that count, but the life in your years. A life without new experiences is like death – there is nothing new anymore. That's perhaps the main difference between a two-year-old and an eighty-two-year-old!

Let us invent a new unit to measure our experience in life – not the chronological one. The unit is "Granny's tales". When you're as old as your grandparents, how many stories will you have to tell your grandchildren? Stories of your exploits and of the fun that you had when you were young? The question is – does every day create a different story or is every day a rerun? It's worth a thought.

Let's look at it another way. If your life is screened on a 24-hour channel, will it be interesting enough? Will you enjoy watching yourself live? For most of us, the answer would be no. Why else would we need movies and TV to entertain us? Can't our life be so interesting and absorbing that we never need to watch another *saas bahu* serial?

Ironically, in spite of knowing that life grows in the moments that are new and unknown, most of us are scared! We are so afraid of trying out the new – be it meeting new people or doing new things – we don't want to create more granny's tales!

So friends, let's emerge from our cocoons and become butterflies that flutter around bravely! Let's have fun and enjoy ourselves – because this time will never come back Let's just live… more life per life!

IN PRACTICE

1. Go through the extra reading article if you still have not done so.
2. List out the new experiences that you can seek – things that you want to do. Writing them gives a lot of energy to your goals.
3. The most important time is when you are about to jump into something new. Keep yourself composed and determined at such times – you will need to.
4. Maintain a track record of the times when you were not assertive, and reward yourself for the times when you actually tried something new.
5. Make this a weekly affair at least.

List of activities done/to be done :

This is very specific to your own life conditions – so make sure you add things to this list as per your situations. Tick each one and reward yourself as and when each one is done.

_____
_____
_____
_____

◆◆

9. Just for Today I Will Spend Some Time in Solitude

People here people there… people, people everywhere! It's a world that's so busy, so very full. Mankind is somehow obsessed with keeping itself preoccupied with something or the other. Check out the infinity of diversions that each one of us has – movies, music, friends, food… the list goes on and on.

The speed at which our lives are moving is alarming. The change that has happened in the last decade is more than the change that happened since mankind came on the planet and up to that decade! There is an information explosion, with every single entity trying really hard to capture your attention and peace of mind.

Speed isn't bad – but excessive speed is. Compare your life with a car that's going at top speed. You may know that the control you have over the car is inversely proportional to the speed – the faster your life goes, the lesser the control you have. Also, when the car is moving at such high speeds, you can hardly see anything out of the window – because of the speed. This implies that as life moves faster, you have lesser and lesser time to enjoy the small joys of life.

If you were to observe your speeding mind, you'll realise that it is hardly sensitive. Speed makes you hard. It makes you impersonal and empty from within. Humans are not made up to cope with change – and that's exactly why we need to spend some time in solitude.

Just as a television beams hundreds of channels, so does your mind keep broadcasting day and night. A TV can be switched off, but very few of us have the ability to switch off the mind. Also, in watching television, you have a remote control that you can switch channels with. But the untrained mind switches channels on its own.

The first step to quieten the mind is to spend time in solitude. When you do so, you will realise how challenging it is. Choose a quiet place to spend at least 30 minutes in complete solitude, with absolutely no disturbance around. No distractions to the mind – for these 30 minutes you must have absolutely nothing to do. No mantras, telephones, TV or computer – absolutely nothing. Take this time to do something that you do rarely – just be.

Initially your mind will be in uproar – and make a lot of noise. You will find thoughts racing at 120 miles per hour! You will feel uneasy and uncomfortable and maybe have an intense desire to speak. But stick to your resolve. The mind that has driven you so often will want to do so again. But when it realises that you, its master, has decided otherwise, it will give up.

It is the nature of the mind to jump from place to place like a monkey. The Buddha said show me two men – one who has conquered a thousand armies of a thousand men each and another who has conquered his mind. The latter shall be far greater! That's how challenging mind control is.

But you will notice that as you spend more time in solitude, you'll feel more energetic afterwards. When your thoughts become still, it lets you go deeper. Just like in a still lake where you can see the bottom, you will come in touch with your deepest being. This won't happen in an instant – it will take time. You will need to have patience. But the rewards are worth it.

People will find you more attentive and receptive. The jobs that you do will become almost perfect. You will experience a feeling of well-being most of the time and become more creative in your thoughts and outlook. All you need to do is start. Practising silence will also empower your intentions – you'll see that what you intend will happen more easily.

There's a saying that I first came across in my school days – and eventually imbibed in my life.

Speech is silvern
Silence is golden!

IN PRACTICE

1. Start with 30 minutes of silence a day – this itself might seem challenging but gradually you will be able to master it.
2. Now gradually increase the time involved – and you will see that the practice becomes almost addictive. Soon, you'll want to spend time in silence.
3. Start watching your thoughts without becoming a part of them. This means that you will not get carried away by your thoughts, but let them come and go. This does not mean blocking your thoughts.
4. Eventually you will notice you become more peaceful. Seek feedback from people to know if you're changing – and be really patient. You will notice that changes definitely come to pass.
5. Pick up every single opportunity to practice silence – it can be mainly when you're waiting for someone or something, or even travelling.

Progress Record

Date	Time	Topic/Dominating Thoughts	Conclusions

◆◆

10. Just for Today I Will Pray for Someone Else

"Be still and know that I am God."

You have a hotline with your creator – do you know what? Prayer! Since childhood, we've been taught to pray. But I am really sure that most of us have forgotten the prayers of gratitude that we'd mugged in our childhood years.

A typical prayer is generally more of asking and less of thanking. I remember reading a prayer: "God, please give me patience and make it fast!!" It seems that in this world of *Yeh dil maange more* (the heart wants more), God has just become a provider and a complaint box. Lots of prayers have the typical why-did-you-do-this-to-me-God?

Everyone prays for himself or herself, and there is no big deal in that. If you've not been praying, you need to start. And yes, there's nothing wrong in asking from God. All that you ask with a clean heart will be provided to you in abundance. But you need to ask.

This reminds me of the story of a child who was walking with his father. On the road he saw a huge stone. Anticipating the fact that it could actually hit someone, the child decided to remove it. He tried really hard, but found it was too heavy. Finally he turned to his father: "Please help me remove this stone."

The father smiled: "I was always there besides you. If only you'd asked earlier."

Prayer is a way of unleashing the Aladdin factor from within you. Aladdin had a lamp, but he had to ask for the wishes – they did not just come to him on their own. Prayer is a way to ask God. But just for today, you will make your prayer unselfish – you'll pray for someone else.

Experientially, I've observed that when someone else prays for you, it comes to pass much faster than what it would normally take. That's the magic of prayer for someone else. When you do that, you're doing it without a selfish motive. That's what makes it so very effective.

Whom do you pray for? Look around and you'll find the answer. There are millions around, the have-nots of the world – starved, deprived, unclothed people who don't even know they must pray. There are so many who are sick and need God's mercy. A small recommendation from you will surely help!

The best form of prayer is the one that comes from instinct and is beyond words. When you're crossing the road and a car approaches you, your mind doesn't frame a sentence, "Please come back, there is a car approaching..." It immediately sends an impulse that pulls you back. So also the greatest form of prayer is through feeling, not words. You'll observe the effect as you get more and more into prayer.

Praying for others is one of the noblest things that we can do as humans. It represents our will to add value to the lives of others and that's what living ultimately is all about. Such prayer also makes you realise how blessed and fortunate you are. Indeed, a true prayer is really powerful.

IN PRACTICE

1. First do a gratitude prayer – thank God for the wonderful gifts of life given to you.
2. Now make a list of people you know who need prayers. Most of the people will fit in. Also make lists of groups of people who need prayers. You can pray for everyone if you wish.
3. Global prayers – praying for the world at large also has an empowering effect on your vision – it will make you feel a part of a much larger family.
4. Pray again before you go to sleep. Bedtime prayers are very effective.
5. Make this a habit.

Progress Record

Person prayed for	Cause	Effect after a month

◆◆

11. Just for Today I Will Treat Everyone I Meet as the Most Important Person in the World

It is nice to be important.

But much more important to be nice.

For each one of us, the centre of our world is ourselves. You are the most important person for yourself, and that is very natural. You are the hero of your life, and all that concerns you is all that's most important to you. But just like you, everyone else considers himself or herself the most important person in the world.

A lot of us have problems in conversing with people. I've seen people get tongue-tied at crucial times, so much so that they can never ever start their conversations. They are at a total loss for words and don't know how to talk. There are other times when people feel too great and arrogant to talk. And in most cases, the conversations are mostly of people who go on talking about themselves.

Dale Carnegie discovered this golden truth in the 1920s – each person loves to talk about himself or herself. When you treat the person you are with as an important person, many things happen. For one, you'll be more open to listening to the person – because you feel the person is important.

This in itself is something really important – people want attention. If there is one precious commodity you can use to build relationships, it's attention. When you make an assumption that the person you're talking to is important, you'll see that the attention flows effortlessly. You will be focussed when the person is talking and s/he will feel at great ease with you.

But why treat the person as the most important one? It is because your mind has an inherent tendency to drive you away from the present. Your thoughts will always dwell on things that are more important. But this will be lesser if you treat the person opposite you as the most important. After all, what can be more important than the most important person in the world?

This simple technique will make you a great conversationalist, and also put others more at ease with you. Each one of us wants to be liked and accepted by others – and this is the best way to make this happen.

I myself had a problem with being a very bad listener. I used to go on and on at the thing I thought I was the best – talking! People who were not close friends would get bored instantly – and why not! Are you too caught up in a similar trap? If so, it's high time you start treating others as important.

The Humanist Brotherhood has a wonderful principle,

Treat others as you yourself would like to be treated.

Wouldn't you too like to be treated as the most important person in the world? Of course! Because you ARE. As you apply this strategy you'll see the number of your friends and acquaintances soar – people will seek you. You'll be liked by a lot of people. All this because you recognise something that they appreciate – the fact that they are important!

Realising this principle will unlock a lot of power. It is a known principle that people behave and respond as per expectations. As a part of this strategy, expect every person to be on his or her best behaviour with you – and you'll see for yourself that it works! It actually happens that people respond to your expectations.

It is important not to do this just for today for results, but simply as an experiment. If you're too concerned about results, you'll become artificial. I'm not asking you to flatter others or give meaningless compliments. Neither am I asking you to lick up to other people. All this strategy needs is a mental attitude that the person who is with you is the most important person in this world.

Try it out today. You'll see the results and conclude that this is perhaps one of the most important chapters in the book!

IN PRACTICE

1. People Scale meter:

    Today when you meet different people, mentally rate them on a scale of one to ten, on the basis of their behaviour towards you. For the best and the most pleasant behaviour you expected, give a 10 and for the worst, 1.

    But wait – there's a catch! What? Simple! Rate each person 10 out of 10. No, you're not trying to kid yourself, but actually creating positive expectations for each person you meet.

2. Become a better listener by not rushing to complete the other person's sentences. This is a major temptation for most of us, but it must be overcome. Also make sure that you ask the right questions that open up the person, rather than interrupting sentences.

3. Give up the "I know it all" look – nothing can be a greater turn-off than that.

4. When you're talking to a person, focus on the person with your eyes as well as ears – body language will betray you if you're doing it artificially.

5. Don't expect this strategy to give overnight results – people will gradually open up to you.

6. Finally, also make sure you appreciate the inner beauty of every person you talk with. This is a very spiritual way to send energy to the person.

Progress Record

Track your current attitude towards the closest people in your life, and see the change after practising this principle.

Person	Current Attitude	New Attitude

◆ ◆

12. Just for Today I Will Smile Ear to Ear

Smile, your everlasting smile, a smile can bring you near to me....
– Boyzone

If there is one universally recognised symbol of happiness and wellbeing, it's the smile. One smile and everyone around you knows that you're happy. Deep within, you find that things are right and feel the joy. A smile can actually be a very important tool to be happy.

Before we launch into that topic, you need to understand what is called the action-emotion connection. When you are happy you smile and when you're sad you frown. It's always been that way, with your body responding to the emotional changes in your mind. But recent studies have presented a very startling fact – that this connection is two-way!

It works both ways basically – not only does action follow emotion, but emotions also follow action. Try this for a moment – droop low with a very sad expression on your face. Frown for some time. Soon you'll feel the emotions creep in too. On the other hand, try acting like you're happy – you'll realise that you soon begin to feel so.

So the action-emotion theory tells us that our emotions can be altered by our body dynamics too. If you act happy, you feel happy.

If you act depressed, you'll feel depressed. If you act peaceful when you're angry, the anger will definitely mellow down.

What does this mean when applied to smiling? It simply means that you don't need to smile when you are happy. But also smile when you're not happy – you'll realise that soon you begin to feel the joy within you. Isn't that a great way to stay happy when you need to?

There's a virtual smile-o-phobia about smiling in our society. The primary question is – if I smile at a stranger, will s/he smile back at me? What if the other person just turns away – or just doesn't like it at all? Forget it, let's not smile!

But such thoughts make absolutely no sense – what is the need for someone to smile back? Your smiling is great enough! You'll realise that gradually you find people who do actually smile back.

Read this beautiful poem on smiling…

SMILE

Smiling is infectious,
you catch it like the flu,
When someone smiled at me today,
I started smiling too.
> I passed around the corner
> and someone saw my grin
> When he smiled I realised
> I'd passed it on to him.

I thought about that smile
then I realised its worth,
A single smile, just like the mind
could travel round the earth.
> So, if you feel a smile begin,
> don't leave it undetected
> Let's start an epidemic quick,
> and get the world infected!

Keep the smile going by sending this on to a friend.
Everyone needs a smile!!!

So don't forget to smile wide – ear to ear. Of course don't apply this all the time – especially when someone else is facing a problem; you could be bashed up for smiling! The best thing is to smile when you are facing a problem – that's being really brave.

Spread the smile virus!!

IN PRACTICE

1. Read some jokes – they will make you laugh or at least smile.
2. We all read comics as kids – so dig out some really good Archies or Tin Tins and read them – it'll be fun.
3. Wear a smile for the day – it'll be the best makeup, making you look really pretty.
4. Put small reminder cards in your wallet, books etc, which say, "SMILE".
5. Watch funny serials and movies.
6. Try to avoid smiling at someone else's expense!

Important

CNN REPORTS A NEW VIRUS HAS RECENTLY BEEN DISCOVERED. ONE PERSON CAN PASS IT ON TO MILLIONS, AS IT IS VERY CONTAGIOUS. THE CENTER FOR DISEASE CONTROL HAS REPORTED THIS WEEK THAT THE VIRUS SPREADS VERY RAPIDLY FROM ONE PERSON TO THE NEXT. THEY HAVE PUT A VERY INTERESTING NAME TO THIS VIRUS.

IT'S CALLED....

A SMILE
UH! OH! TOO LATE! I SEE IT ON YOUR FACE ALREADY!
You've got the virus!!!

◆◆

13. Just for Today I Will Take Care of My Body

The body is said to be the temple of the soul – and most often, this temple is more ignored than anything else. Look at your own body for a moment – do you take sufficient care of it? If you were to observe carefully, in most cases the answer would be 'No'. We are really used to abusing our bodies.

Do I see you shaking your head? Body abuse and me? No way! Let me tell you how do you do it. Whenever you eat something that your body finds hard to digest – meat, oils and refined flour products – it's abuse. These take much more time to digest and your poor body often goes nuts digesting them.

Look at your teeth – if you're like most others, you have a minor problem that you've not referred to the dentist as yet. A majority of us brush or floss incorrectly. And trust me, dental problems are the most common in the world, after the common cold, of course. I learnt it the hard way. After postponing my visit to the dentist for years, I began suffering toothaches and it soon became unbearable. As a result of my procrastination, I had to get four teeth extracted – three premolars and one molar. I couldn't chew at all for some time. The reason? Ignoring the body.

We all believe that if something is ignored, it will cease to exist. But this is not true in the case of your body. If your body has some pain or abnormality, you have to treat it as an action signal. It means that something has gone wrong, or is about to. It means that there is something your body is trying to tell you and you need to listen.

Care for your body also includes general cleanliness. Most of us ignore certain areas when we bathe – like the back of our ears, back of the knees, webs between the toes etc. Remember, cleanliness is next to Godliness. It is a must to become clean in order to stay healthy.

Another problem of our generation is the large-scale sensory abuse that we indulge in. Be it a teenager listening to music at 140 decibels and damaging his ears, or a housewife watching television from a distance of a few feet – it's all a sure way of damaging these precious sensory organs in the long run.

I also hope you're reading this book in the right posture. If not, you're not only causing eyestrain but also bending your backbone into funny shapes. If that's the case, straighten into the right posture – now! It is also not a good habit to read while lying down.

How can you take care of your body? The first step is to rectify the general mistakes we make daily. I've already pointed out many of them to you, so you should be able to take corrective action. The whole problem is that these faults will not show up immediately. But in the long run they will successfully create everlasting problems.

Make sure you have checkups regularly – it is best to detect a problem in its early stages than wait for it to grow into a full-blown one. Ignoring a problem is the best way to make it worse. Dental, eye and body checkups are preventions that are much better than cures. It's better to kill the monster while it is still small.

The second component to taking care of your body is to keep track of the inputs into your body. Vedic traditions lay special emphasis on food for the simple reason that ultimately you are what you eat. 98% of your body will be replaced within a year! So what you eat is what you get. But this rule doesn't apply only to the actual food. What you're feeding your senses is equally important. What you see, hear, smell and touch are as important. The mind and body being inseparably linked, this becomes equally important.

Every input creates a bodily reaction – so closely monitor what goes in.

Finally, make sure you love your body. Pamper it, and you'll see the fun. I've outlined techniques for the same in the In Practice section of this chapter. I'm sure you'll enjoy pampering yourself, and giving self-love. There are many times when we're harsh on ourselves – let's start loving ourselves before we can actually love others!

IN PRACTICE

1. Take a full body massage sometime – it is a great way to pamper yourself.
2. Self-love is also fun. Rub your palms together and starting from the head, touch every part of your body giving it love and mentally expressing gratitude to it. Do this till you come to your toes; you can repeat this.
3. The same exercise can also be done with a partner – make the partner lie down and give him or her a motherly touch. Make sure you choose the partner carefully!
4. Take a long bath today – take twice the time you do, paying attention to each part of your body as you clean it. Give it love and mentally express gratitude as you wash it
5. Be aware of what you eat today. When you're confused, just ask yourself if your body needs it, and whether it will actually nourish you. Then decide whether to eat it or not.
6. Be aware of the sensory inputs that you have – they are also crucial.

♦♦

14. Just for Today I Will Spend Time with Nature

What is life, so full of care?

We have no time to stand and stare!!

Never before have these words rung more true than now. Mankind is caught up in an endless web of working and achieving more and more. The Buddha had said that desire is the root cause of all sorrow. In a world where advertisements constantly fan the fires of this desire, we are not heading anywhere.

One of the best ways to slow down a fast life is to observe nature. Living in concrete jungles has made us so very used to the man-made artificial world that we seldom stop to stand and stare. Who has the time anyway? Smelling a fresh flower or playing with a butterfly…. the most enjoyable moments I've ever spent are amidst natural beauty.

You can spend time with anything that's natural. It can be a sunrise or a sunset that you simply observe. You can spend time gazing at the moon. Take a long walk on the seashore and just watch the waves come and go by. Or go to some place with plenty of trees. If that is not possible, observe the birds and plants around you. Even in the most crowded cities, at least some signs of natural beauty will be there.

What exactly does this mean? It implies spending time in solitude – not bothering to think about anything else. Leave the rest of the world behind and spend some time with yourself. Don't do anything else when you're in the company of nature – no watching TV, listening to music or reading. Just be there.

I realised how difficult this was when I gave this tip to one of my students. He was really addicted to the television, so I told him to spend some time observing greenery and trees. When things didn't improve for a month or so I decided to investigate, only to find that he was watching more of the National Geographic channel! His idea of spending time with nature was watching more nature-based programmes on TV! Remember, there is absolutely no substitute for the real thing.

What happens when you spend time with nature? Firstly, and most importantly, your mind slows down. In a life that's running at such a high pace, it's always advisable to slow down a bit, and reflect on what is going on. Such reflections are best done in nature.

I have myself observed that when amidst natural surroundings, your thought patterns are completely different. Your thoughts, you'll observe, are clearer and more focussed. You will be able to relate to circumstances easily, and make sense out of what is happening. You will also be thinking positive and optimistic. Such is the power of nature!

The best of this is when you go into the Himalayas. If you've still not been to the grand mountains of India, you're missing a lot. You need to explore and look around. You will see that when you're there, you're in total bliss. It's the vibrations, or the energy of that place that draws you towards it. It is really magical!

When you're in tune with nature's intelligence, your thoughts will slow down. Consequently, you'll move much closer to your inner self. You will tend to become more loving and caring. You will also get more intuitive. Your intentions will become empowered and driven. Indeed, nature's magic is wonderful!

When you're into it, you can try what I do to feel better. When I'm in any natural surroundings, I focus all my attention on the beauty of the object. I look at its shape and colour, and it actually begins to stand out. I breathe in the beauty, and the feeling it gives is awesome. It makes me feel invincible, as if everything in my life is going right. It energises me beyond expectations.

If you think that a place of natural beauty is far from where you live, you're wrong. If you look around, you'll find lots of natural stuff to observe and appreciate. If nothing, at least the sun and the moon are around!

IN PRACTICE

1. Look around your city for any nature clubs – these associations generally have a great knowledge about the surroundings and places.
2. Every month, take a holiday of at least two days, preferring natural destinations to man-made ones.
3. Long walks near the sea are a great way to relax. Salt water in fact destroys all negative energy, and makes you feel much better.
4. Mornings are the best time to observe nature. Just when the sun is about to rise, the world wears a different hue with birds chirping merrily and leaves rustling in the wind. It's divine! Try and capture this moment.
5. Even when you're not amidst total greenery or natural beauty, you can still look for trees and birds, savouring their beauty.
6. Hill-stations a great places to spend quality time with nature. It's an investment that will make you much stronger.

Listing your favourite places

List your favourite places and make plans to visit them – they need not be far, but as close as the garden round the corner too!

Place	Plan to Visit

◆◆

15. Just for Today I Will Keep an Open Mind

Minds are like parachutes,
They function only when open.

The human organism has one remarkable quality – it tends to learn from the past. Nature has equipped us with this cybernetic loop that makes sure we always recall our experiences and use them to evaluate similar situations in the future. That is how we learn and grow.

But there are times when this very quality becomes a problem! In childhood if you were chased by a ferocious dog, for example, this will be stored in your memory. This will make you believe that all dogs are dangerous. So the next time you approach a dog, you'll feel fearful. Even if the dog is friendly, your past conditioning will not allow you to accept this fact.

Look at this picture of a man playing a saxophone. Can you see something else too?

Your mind is conditioned to look at black on white, so you see the man. However, if you try to look at white on a black background you'll notice the silhouette of a girl. That's how your past conditioning can actually prevent you from seeing the truth!

When something new is registered in the mind, it tends to compare this with the information it already has in store. If it is in sync with that, the mind will accept it. If it is not, your mind will reject it. That's how old beliefs get stronger. When you look at someone really old, you'll find that it is very difficult for people to change their beliefs, simply because they are so deep rooted.

So just for today, you'll be open to new ideas and look at them objectively. When you receive a suggestion, don't just discount it right away. Look at it and try and see what the other person is trying to tell you. You may actually end up discovering a very precious treasure!

Also make sure that you don't defend mistakes or beliefs. It is very tempting to tell the other person, "You are wrong!" But it doesn't help much. You yourself might be at the wrong end, so put yourself under the critical eye first, and then react.

Keeping your mind open has a spiritual component to it too. It involves looking for coincidences. Basically, no event in your life is a mere coincidence, but it has a deeper meaning to it. So if you have an intuition, display the guts to follow it. If you think you know a person, try and connect to the person. Be open to the way events are moving, for they will lead you somewhere. A very beautiful book on this subject is *The Celestine Prophecy* by James Redfield.

Just for today, you will also not force your way of things – let things move the way they are. Learn to go with the flow, rather than trying to go against it, and wanting your way to happen. Accept other ideas, opinions and decisions – it's just for today.

Keeping an open mind is the best way to grow – you learn such a lot from things and events around you. This is a way to evolve spiritually. Remember, a closed mind is like a closed parachute. It is of no use, and a big burden on your back!

IN PRACTICE

1. Remain defenceless and don't argue. Let the other person's viewpoint prevail too. There can be more than one person who is right at the same time.
2. Look for coincidences in the events of the day, and try to interpret them. They will surely reveal some deeper meaning.
3. Don't force your viewpoint on others; let them hold theirs, as you do yours. Let it be mutual.
4. Let go of your past conditioning, trying to look at things from a new and fresh perspective. This will ensure that your innocence returns.

◆◆

16. Just for Today I Will Decide to Remain Happy

Happiness is the ultimate goal of all mankind – look at all your actions for any given day. You can classify them into two parts – one to gain pleasure and the other to avoid pain. Look at what you're doing in life right now. It ultimately boils down to a search for happiness – who doesn't want to be happy?

I am reminded of an interesting anecdote on happiness. A street urchin was happily sitting on the footpath, doing nothing.

"What are you doing here? You're wasting your time you fool! You must do something worthwhile?" a passerby remarked.

"What do you think I must do, oh revered master?"

"Do some work – get employed somewhere, rather than doing nothing at all."

"What will happen then?" the urchin enquired.

"You'll have some money to live by," the passerby said.

"And what will I do with the money?" the urchin wanted to know.

"You'll be able to live a better life – have a home, marry and have kids!" the passerby was getting impatient.

"And then?" persisted the urchin.

"You'll be happy and enjoy your life!" The passerby was sure he'd convinced the urchin. But the reply he got put all his doubts to rest.

The urchin responded with a smile: "Be happy and enjoy my life? That's what I'm doing even now!"

Not that I'm asking you to become like the street urchin, wasting time doing nothing. The aim of the story is to illustrate the fact that happiness is not the way we look at. It's much different from this, and understanding it will help us know better.

Most us think or look at happiness as a destination. We make statements like: I'll be happy when….

I earn X amount of money

When everyone loves me

When I get that gizmo

After I finish my world tour

On being promoted to_____.

What you need to realise is that you don't need a reason to be happy. What will be the difference when you achieve these targets? Only that you will give yourself the permission to be happy! You'll let yourself experience happiness only then. Do you see the folly?

The happiness you're seeking is not something external – it's very much within you. Except that you've made certain rules regarding when you will 'let yourself be happy'. Modify these rules and happiness will be easier to achieve. Break them, and you'll be happy forever.

One of the most beautiful "rules of happiness" is from one of my friends. He says that every morning he feels a rush of happiness as soon as he gets up. How? Says my friend: "I'm alive and on Earth – isn't that a great reason to be happy!" With a rule like that you'll surely be happy for a long, long time to come.

You need to realise that happiness is a decision – you can decide to be happy. Once you do that and your decision is strong enough, no one can change that. You need to have that strong resolve. Just for today, mentally make a decision that you'll remain happy irrespective of the circumstances. Make that decision now.

Once you've made this decision, congratulate yourself. You deserve a pat on your back! But wait. You need to be strong enough to stick to this decision. Don't let circumstances or events spoil the wonderful resolution that you've made. This will happen from a consciousness that you are ultimately responsible for all your happiness and grief.

IN PRACTICE

1. Examine your happiness rules – I'll be happy when
_____
_____
_____

2. Look at reasons that you have to be happy
_____
_____
_____

3. Put down your decision to be happy on paper right here :

On_____<date> I,_____
<name> resolve to be happy throughout the day, come what may!
Signature _____

4. List the times/reasons that upset you or could have upset you.
_____
_____
_____
_____

◆◆

17. Just for Today I Will Spend Some Time Thinking

I am going to give you a very interesting suggestion – to spend some time thinking. At the same time I realise that I risk sounding really ridiculous. Thinking? That's what we do all the time! How can I have this as my Just for Today??? No way! It's just not possible!

Before you jump to conclusions, it will be wise to look at our thinking first. All day, your mind keeps beaming like a television. There is a constant flow of thoughts, each one leading to another. There are, however, two major differences between the TV and the mind.

While for TV you have the remote control, your mind changes channels on its own.

In case of the TV you can just turn it off, but you aren't powerful enough to do that to your mind.

So basically the mind is a dangerous TV, if left uncontrolled. Thinking, as you will see, is very self-feeding – it continues as a long link, with one thought connected to another. It goes on and on till you realise that you're caught in the thought trap. And that itself, being another thought, makes you go on another ride. Such is the magic of the mind!

If you've experienced a mind race, you'll realise the danger of a speeding thought process. You will see that there are times when thoughts just refuse to stop. It's almost as if your mind has been connected to some high-powered battery where thoughts are racing at the speed of light. You want to take control, but the thoughts are so overpowering that they speed right ahead.

With all this, how can I ask you to spend some time thinking? There's a difference here. What I am proposing is you do conscious thinking on a subject. Don't be guided by your mind and thoughts. Instead, try to focus on the topic that you're thinking about.

You will need the aid of a pen and a paper to do "conscious thinking" and pen down your thoughts. Pick up a topic that you're almost obsessed with and think about most of the time. In my case at one point of time, it was my college festival.

I wanted to head the college festival and was virtually obsessed by it. It was a really challenging time. The first thoughts that I'd get even before going to the loo would be of the fest. When I'd lie on the bed, I'd spend endless hours with my thoughts just racing. And the sad part was that most of the thoughts were repetitive. I desperately needed to break free, and decided that the time was NOW.

I have always had a habit of writing down whatever I think. So I did a conscious thinking session and sat down at an isolated place. I started brainstorming and asking myself questions, jotting down the answers and the most recurring thoughts. For almost two hours I was scribbling. But at the end of it, I was relieved! I had dumped my thoughts on paper, and they just left my mind, making place for newer thoughts.

You can pick up any problem, life situation or something that doesn't directly concern you. Then do the steps I've outlined and have a conscious thinking session. Many people at first experience a thought blackout. They get no thoughts! How wonderful – the state of thoughtlessness is here! But the main cause behind this is that your mind has learnt to disobey you conveniently.

The use of this technique is to discipline the mind. As you know, the greatest challenge we've faced is that of mind control. It is very difficult to control the mind. And that is what thinking consciously makes you do.

This wonderful habit will help you think forward instead of just moving in circles. Isn't that something to think about??

IN PRACTICE

1. List out five topics/areas/problems that you can think about:
_____
_____
_____

2. Keep a thinking journal – record your thoughts there.

Thinking Session
    Date   :
    Time   :
    Place   :
    Thought topic :
    Thoughts   :

3. Conclusions drawn.

◆◆

18. Just for Today I Will Do Some Mental Exercises

Your mind and body are inseparably connected. In fact, quantum physics says that your body is nothing but a manifestation of your thoughts. Similarly, a lot of diseases may be traced to your mind – specifically the thoughts that you think will decide and have their reactions on your body. This influence is something that has to be accepted and used, for even science is now recognising it.

Just like the body needs exercise, so does the mind. It is no exception. Imagine you can see your mind as a human being – how would it be? What would its physique be like? Would it be really strong like say, Arnold Schwarzeneggar? Or would it be very slim, trim and flexible? This depends on your thinking and use of the mind.

The simple rule that applies here is – *use it or lose it*. Your mind has infinite power. In fact, the number of connections in your mind is a number so large that it has baffled scientists so often. It has been discovered that to make a supercomputer as powerful as the human mind, with the current technology it would take space equal to the Empire State Building! That is the immense power of your brain.

But your mind needs exercise. Just as the body can be exercised in a number of ways – weights, athletics, gymnastics or swimming – the mind too can be exercised in different ways for each of its faculties. This will make that particular faculty of mind more potent. Intelligence is genetic – it is inherent. But it can be developed too. Research has shown that education and training have a far greater impact on it than genetics can ever have.

Exercising the mind means doing any of these activities that challenge your thinking and make you use those grey cells. A few I can suggest are:
1. Solving a crossword
2. Reading something challenging
3. Trying to solve a problem
4. Doing mathematics
5. Solving riddles, anagrams etc.

Basically you will see that anything that challenges your mental muscles also builds them up. Uselessly gaping at the TV or playing endless hours of video games is no way to make this happen – and be warned, such garbage fed into your brain can make it extremely dull and inactive. Your mental exercises need to be challenging.

I remember the case of one of my patients who had a very lazy brain. When I recommended mental exercises and he tried them, he was overwhelmed with the amount of pressure on his brain. He said he was mentally exhausted – maybe something similar to the kind of pain you experience when you first exercise.

But there is a major difference. Physical exercises produce acids, release toxins and make you tired. That is absolutely inevitable because it is a bodily process. However, there are no such secretions during mental activity. Which means that getting mentally tired is only an illusion – nothing more than that! YOU CAN GO ON WORKING INDEFINITELY MENTALLY – It's all in the mind, you see!

Let me give you the example of a pencil – it's fun to write only when it is sharp and pointed. Similarly, mental exercises will sharpen your mind – they will make it more useable. When sunlight is concentrated at one place with the help of a convex glass, it results in fire! That is the power of concentration and focus, which you can tap by training your mind.

As you train your mind, you'll be able to solve problems more easily. Your level of common sense will also increase – and so will your ability to remember things. And all these skills are more acquired than genetic. Your brain is very elastic. It depends on how much you stretch it.

IN PRACTICE

1. Do the mental exercises I've listed in this chapter and see how well you do them.
2. Visualisation is an important mental faculty – how developed it is also counts. Try one visualisation exercise where you try to see something with your mind's eye.
3. Try numerical exercises too – like counting backwards, doubling a number on and on, reciting tables backwards etc.
4. Recommended books here are the Mental Exercise Book, and other mind power books.
5. Also eat foods that supplement your thinking, and drink plenty of water.
6. If you have to watch the TV, please watch some intellectually stimulating programmes.

◆◆

19. Just for Today I Will Give and be Open to Receiving

Give, and thou shalt receive

Look at the world around you – and you'll see that you've been almost brainwashed into wanting. Wanting more and more. Our ads and the media have all made you believe that you can't be happy till you have that particular product or service. You've been made the wanting kid.

When I began studying economics, I had read that: "Human wants are unlimited". Today I see the truth of that statement more than ever before. If a modern man gets Aladdin's lamp, his first wish will be some possession he doesn't have – like a car or a computer. For his second wish he may ask for a big home or a place of fame. But I'm sure that for the third wish, he will ask for three more wishes!

We've all heard the cliché: "True joy is in giving", but never really experienced it. If you were to, you'd see how true it is. Before going into details on the topic of giving, you need to understand how to give. That is an art in itself!

When you are giving, the most important thing is the intention behind the act – why are you giving? If the act of giving makes you feel at a loss, it is of no benefit. True giving is for joy – it is for understanding the needs of others and trying to fulfill them. When you give and feel happy thereafter, you will see what I mean.

India has been a land of generosity. King Harsha Vardhan once gave away his own jewellery and clothing when donating to the people! And there was Karna, who would give whatever was asked for, and even gave his protective shield that had afforded him invincibility! Such is the greatness of giving.

You need to be a giver to experience that joy – and you can start right away. There are people all around you whom you can give something or the other of lasting value. When you add value to their lives they will add value to yours. When you give, you receive.

This universe too operates on circulation – where there is no circulation, there is suffocation. Look at your own body, for example. It is constantly taking in oxygen and giving out carbon dioxide. Your blood is constantly flowing through you. If this flow were to be blocked, it would create problems within you. Try tying a string tightly to one of your fingers and restrict the blood flow – it will soon get discoloured and cold. Over a long time, it will lose sensation too.

It is a universal law that anything that stagnates, degenerates. Likewise, you need to keep circulating. What you give need not be expensive. Look at Sudama, who took three fistfuls of rice for his friend Lord Krishna. But he gave. It is the act itself that counts.

Forget the cost and the gift needn't be material too, it can merely be a thought. You can mentally pray for the person, or send him blessings. Even these are acts of giving.

When you give, you create a vacuum in you – and nature abhors a vacuum. So more will flow into your life. Tithe – giving 10 percent of your earnings to the church – is a great way to keep the circulation of money going. Start giving today and you'll see the dynamic flow that you set in motion. Only ensure that when you give, you give it with a grateful heart and with an intention to benefit the other person.

The other component to giving is receiving. You will see that when you start giving, gifts will pour into your life too. One word of caution though – don't expect this to happen, and don't give for this reason! However, when gifts do come your way, accept them with grace. Be open to receiving too. Such circulation will make you spiritually healthy too! And remember, there is more than enough for all of us in this universe.

IN PRACTICE

1. Just for today, try to give to every person you come across. It can be anything small like a flower, or a chocolate, but try to give with a grateful heart.
2. If you can't give anything material, you can at least mentally pray for the person. Maybe you can give a compliment too.
3. Circulate wealth – be free to giving money. Do it with the intention of benefiting the other person, and not grudgingly.
4. Also be open to receiving gifts from the universe or everyone around you.
5. At the end of the day, make a list of what you consciously gave and got. You'll be surprised!

Progress Records

Date	Gifts Received	From

This list will actually make you realise the value of each gift that you receive but have never ever taken notice of.

♦ ♦

20. Just for Today I Will Spread the Love

It's love that makes the world go round!

The most noble of emotions that man experiences is that of love – when you love, you can truly be your higher self. Love also brings out the best in others. Look at a mother who loves her child, or a lover who longs for his beloved. Love is universal, but what I suggest is that it must become a universal currency!

One of my gurus is Sri Sri Ravi Shankar, who is an embodiment of divine love. One look at his photograph will make you smile. His presence will make you feel the warmth within – this is one man who radiates love. Similar experiences have been reported to me on seeing other spiritual gurus like Satya Sai Baba, Asaram Bapu and Osho Rajneesh. This is simply because these people have learnt to spread the love.

If you've experienced love, you'll know how pure it makes you. The feeling is that of perfection and invincibility. It is complete bliss and joy; indeed that is the power of love!

If that's the magic of love, it's something very odd,
For it makes you feel that someone is almost like God!

However, what you must have been experiencing up to now is selective love – felt only for your loved ones, relatives and friends. What I suggest is something more and different from this – it is to love universally. It is to love everyone without any prejudice or preconceived notions. Just love for the sake of it, for love that you have inherent within you, for your fellow beings.

Such love is also very unconditional. If you look at love these days, it has become more of a commercial deal. If you do this I'll love you and if you do that I will not! It's subject to conditions – and I think it is more of a power struggle. That's how the so-called magic of love fades, and relationships get spoilt.

When the master was asked by one of his disciples on how he could get that magic back into his love, the master said, "Ask as a favour what you had been claiming as a right up to now!" How true! That's the small difference that makes a big difference. Love is all about unconditional acceptance rather than changing people.

Universal love, as I said, means love for all. Just for today, fill yourself with love, and project that love to all. Talk to everyone lovingly, and forgive their mistakes. Just like a mother, who may scold a child momentarily, but will never ever want to harm the child. That's the kind of love you need.

You will know you have it when others see a perennial twinkle in your eyes and a smile on your face. When others feel extremely comfortable in your company. It's nothing that can be taught – but yes, it is always possible to experience it.

Hugging is something that we are so hesitant about doing – but it's a beautiful way of expressing love. Most of us don't even get one hug in a day; but we need at least three for well-being and the ideal is 12! So start a hugging war – hug each other whenever you meet.

True love will fill every moment of your existence with vibrance and wonder. That's the magic of love!

IN PRACTICE

1. Just for today, feel yourself filled with love, like a balloon.
2. Whenever you meet someone, mentally project love to them.
3. Hug your loved ones – you need a minimum number of hugs per day – three at least!
4. Just for today, don't try to change people – love them unconditionally.

Some quotes on love:
It is love, not reason, that is stronger than death.   –Thomas Mann
Love is like a violin. The music may stop now and then, but the strings remain forever.
–Anonymous
Truly loving another means letting go of all expectations. It means full acceptance, even celebration of another's personhood.
–Anonymous
A person can be in love with someone forever till the end of time. But if that person doesn't tell or show the feelings of love, it will be just another person living in a dream, lost of true love.
–Anonymous
Love is the irresistible desire to be irresistibly desired.
–Anonymous
Expression of Love is Service
Expression of Joy is your Smile
Expression of Peace is Meditation
Expressing God is Conscious Action
Think about these lines to comprehend one of the greatest powers of the universe – love!   ◆ ◆

21. Just for Today I Will Have Faith in Myself

Whenever I talk about faith, I have a very interesting story that comes to my mind. It's about what is done in rural India to elephants. On one of my journeys to southern India, I noticed something very interesting. Elephants were tied with thin ropes. Now the same elephants were engaged to pick up huge logs of wood. The surprising part was that the elephants never ever tried to break the frail rope that held them captive. Was it that they wanted to be bonded? No!

A local revealed the answer to this riddle to me. It is a great example of what lack of belief and faith can do. When the elephant was just born, it was tied to the tree with this rope. At that time it did not have the strength to break the rope. It would try many times, but would not succeed. In the end, the elephant gave up. It was pointless to try and fail again. But as the elephant grew, its strength increased, but not its belief. It would still believe that the rope was unbreakable, and as a result never try!

If there is one person whom we tend to underestimate the most, it's ourselves. We are so used to not believing in our abilities, that in the end we tend to achieve much less. It is said that you must shoot for the moon. Even if you miss, you'll land among the stars. Are you shooting for the moon? I don't think so.

. There are many times in a day when you need to make a decision based on your abilities. You need to decide, say whether you can accomplish a particular task or not. At such times, what counts most is the faith that you have in yourself. It's how much you believe you can do that counts the most. Sadly, most of us end up making conservative choices.

If you were to observe, such choices are based on your past experiences. If you've failed in the past or it is something you've never done, you'll tend to avoid it. Not making mistakes comes from experience. But ironically, experience comes from making plenty of mistakes! So if you don't try something out of fear, you'll lose the experience. You'll thus not develop the particular ability, and in the end, the lack of that ability will breed even more fear in you. That's the vicious circle that we're looking at breaking.

Having faith in yourself is all about knowing your limits first. You need to know what you're good at and what you're not. This you'll know only from trying. I can ask you, for example, if you're good at opera singing. You'll say you're not. But the point is, have you tried it yet? If you haven't, how can you say you're good or bad at it?

Having faith in yourself comes from the realisation that you can always learn from something you don't succeed at. Anything that hurts, instructs! It's all about being confident in life, and trying newer things. Trust me, you're capable of much more than what you actually try to do!

Faith can move mountains. Today, all over the world, people are accomplishing miracles that are almost unexplainable by science – accomplished solely on faith. I am reminded of people who have cured diseases like breast cancer, when all of medical science had given up. The only tool that they had was faith. And what a powerful tool! It made things possible. Today and as you read this, faith healing systems are gaining increasing acceptance all over the world.

People have accomplished miracles on the strength of faith, and faith alone. What do you think must have been Columbus' thoughts when he first sailed west? Would it be about fear of all the problems that he was expecting? No! It would be about faith – that someday he would find land. And he did!

Faith in God ultimately boils down to faith in yourself. All that you need is within. You have all the powers it takes to be a mystic. Faith merely channelises them so that you can accomplish miracles. All the great men in this world are biologically like you and me. But one thing that distinguishes them is the faith that they have had.

When you have faith, let it be without any doubt. Let it be totally unconditional. A faith that is in the presence of a hidden, lurking fear will never work – it will only make things worse. Let your faith be without any doubt, and in the end it will yield results.

One very important component to faith is that it is based on the experiences that you've had, and chosen to focus on. Say, you play a game ten times, and win eight of them. Now if you will remember the two that you lost, you'll feel like a loser. You'll not have faith in yourself. On the other hand, focus on the other eight, and you'll see how dramatically it increases your confidence. While performing, the most successful people have held thoughts of their most successful moments in mind. That's one of the secrets of success, for the mind has a tendency to attract such events to itself.

What happens when you have faith in yourself? Your self-confidence makes other people attracted to you. You become more open to newer ideas, for you know they will only add to your pool of knowledge. You will not fear trying out newer experiences and learn from them.

The most important thing is to know what you can do well, and have faith in yourself that you can really do it well. True knowledge lies in knowing the extent of one's limitations and abilities. Have faith and you will be able to accomplish even the most challenging tasks, but without self-confidence, even the smallest hurdles will seem like mountains.

IN PRACTICE

1. For today, you will examine tasks that you are good at. Try doing them and improve.
2. Whenever a decision comes that requires you to trust your abilities do so without hesitation. Not making mistakes is a greater crime!
3. Use selective memory – when you are recalling anything, try and focus on the positives only. If you do that, you'll be able to perform better. Don't get affected by failure, for it's only an indication of the future success that is to come. Your belief will build on the strength of positive experiences.
4. Praying to God and having faith in an external object is equally helpful. Even if you do that, it will channelise your inner powers.
5. Finally, examine the quality of your faith – is it unconditional? Is it without any hesitation or fear? If not, refine your faith.

Exercise

Try this exercise to strengthen your belief systems.
Belief Desired: I am a great student.

Events to support the belief:
1. Secured 88.66% in SSC.
2. Achieved the target of 84% in HSC.
3. Highest in Economics in college.
4. Need the least time to study.
   [add your own reasons to support the belief]

People who think so:
1. Mummy
2. My Father
3. Akanksha, my sister
4. Hemang, my best friend

This should work on strengthening your belief

◆◆

22. Just for Today I Will Act in Congruency

One of the greatest secrets to living a wonderful life is acting in congruency. It is that key which has virtually opened many doors of joy for me. Just for today, you are to experience one of the best insights that I've ever had in life – the insight of acting in congruency!

What does one mean by congruency? Remember geometry – where you learnt that if any two figures are the same in shape and size, they are said to be congruent. Two things are congruent when they are exactly the same. What has geometry to do with spirituality and living better? A lot, if you ask me.

We shall apply the same principle of congruency in our daily lives too. Applied to life, congruency simply means that your mind and body go in the same direction. What you have in your mind is exactly what you act on and act as. Sounds too simple?

Arjuna as a child was being trained under the great Dronacharya. The teacher was imparting a lesson in archery. He asked all his students to aim at a parrot sitting on the tree. Once his students had done that, he asked Bheem what he could see. Bheem replied that he could see the tree and the river next to it.

Similarly, Duryodhan said that he could see the sky and the clouds. None of them were focused on the parrot.

But when Dronacharya asked Arjuna, he had his reply – all that Arjuna could see was the parrot's eye! What do you think would be the result of Arjuna's shot? In all probability, it would hit the target – because of the congruency between his mind and body. If we compare this to the kind of life we're living today, it would almost be as if we are aiming at the parrot, looking at the fruit, and thinking of the fish! That's the kind of life we live!

What you need is to focus your mind on the task that you have in hand. Focus your entire attention on that task, and cut yourself out from the rest of the world. Let there be no interruptions, no distractions. This not only applies to studies, but also to many other things, like eating, for example. I've seen people watch TV while eating – neither can they eat, nor can they watch TV wholeheartedly.

Whenever my mother asks me to do something, she's surprised at two things – the quality of the job and the speed at which I do it. I have a simple secret – acting in focus, in congruency. As soon as I'm given a task, for the time that I am doing it, I act as if it is the most important task in the world. It is focused concentration that brings such results.

Students often complain to me that they can't concentrate on things. I too remember attending some really boring lectures during my school days. Each one of us would be physically present in the school. But mentally, each was on a flight of fancy. I'm sure if you'd be able to see those mental images, you'd get nothing short of a world tour! With this, there was hardly any congruency, any focus, and naturally the results were poor.

To achieve congruency, it is extremely important to do only one thing at a time. With the advent of computers and Windows, my life got really simplified. But I developed the habit of doing many tasks at a time – each in a hurry. When I analysed it, I realised that I caught it from my computer, where I could do many different things at a single time. The disastrous consequences were that I started doing so all the time!

How does one achieve that state of mind? It all depends on where your senses are at that moment. And it doesn't take much to distract your already hyperactive, inattentive mind! When you're doing something, try to focus all your senses on it. Your thinking and thoughts come mainly from your senses, and you'll manage to stay focussed longer with your sensory inputs in place.

Congruency can give you the most amazing benefits, especially if you make it a way of life. In almost every aspect of life, acting this way is beneficial. Everywhere the mind and body are focussed and that makes a powerful combination that brings powerful changes.

For example, if you eat with full congruency, what will the result be? It will be that you'll focus more on the food. You will be able to experience its taste better. You'll chew it more fully and look at it well before you take it in. And all this will make your digestion much stronger. As a result, you'll stay more energetic and focused!

Thus, let's start making this a way of life.

IN PRACTICE

1. Meditation is the best way to bring your mind to calm and focus it on the task. Learn to meditate from some centre around you – any form of meditation, if pursued diligently, will get you results.
2. Eating an orange – try this exercise to improve your experience of eating an orange. Before you start to eat it, see it with complete attention. Feel its skin and smell it. Now very slowly peel it and take a slice. Smell it and slowly put it in your mouth. Try to hear yourself chew it, but don't make sounds while doing that! Complete eating the orange in this way and you'll discover flavours you'd never before experienced.
3. Many times during the day, just ask yourself if you're focussed on the task at hand. If you are, go on. But just in case you're not, focus your attention and continue.
4. If there is something that seems almost impossible to focus your attention on, give yourself a break. Do something that you enjoy and then come back to that activity.
5. Apply this strategy to various life situations, and see the results.

◆◆

23. Just for Today I Will Live in the Present

The past is history,
The future – a mystery,
But this moment is a gift…
So it is called "present"

How wonderfully do these lines describe the essence of joyful living! A mantra for being perpetually happy is hidden in these words. Even if we follow this alone, we can remain happy forever!

The mantra is: BE IN THE PRESENT. Enjoy this moment. Life is a journey where you are not sure of your destination. So why wait for the destination that is not even known, and leave our happiness to it? Let us enjoy the present. The journey of life itself. Why not forget our past guilts and future worries, to enjoy the present moment and experience it to the fullest?

The mind is a machine programmed to misbehave. This happens most of the time, as our mind is out of our own control. We cannot do what we ourselves feel, but are rather driven by the desires of the mind. Said Buddha, "Show me two men, one who has defeated a thousand armies and one who has controlled his mind, and I'll consider the latter much greater!" Even a hero like Arjuna found it difficult to get his mind under his control. So great is the challenge of controlling the mind.

Now this very mind has a monkey-like tendency to jump to either the future or the past without any rhyme or reason, at the very first opportunity. And this flow of thoughts is beyond our control. We need to train our mind to be focussed. Meditation helps a lot and the most common form has been described at the end of this chapter. However, if we are completely focussed on doing the job of the present moment, every task is a meditation in itself.

How easy it seems! Once we do this, not only will our life be entirely free of struggles, but every job will also be a joy and a work of art. Participate in any activity with total attention and you will see that the quality of work shows a marked improvement and is more satisfying. Every task then becomes a meditation. Always remember to be into the task one hundred percent. When you are talking, let the words come from your heart. When you are eating, think of nothing but the food. Look at it with your eyes, smell it and feel it. Enjoy its taste and chew it thoroughly. Then even eating will be an art.

Another very important aspect of this law is the matching of your thoughts and actions. You might have expected a very positive result out of something but in the end it turned out terrible. What went wrong? Didn't you align your thinking in a positive direction? Didn't you hope for the best? Then why did this happen?

This happened because your thoughts and actions didn't match. Once you have decided to do something, apply yourself to it fully. Leave no stone unturned to achieve it. Give your best shot to every game. This is not only for the Herculean tasks in your life but also for every small thing, like preparing tea, or playing a game. This is very similar to being in congruency.

Your mind most of the time moves into the past or the future – let's examine these things from an objective point of view. What is the past? It is nothing but a track of memories of events – real or imagined – that have happened to you. Your past exists nowhere except in your mind – as chemical traces of memory, which can be altered. Of course, it's a different thing that when we are into it, the past seems so real.

Similarly, the future is nothing but an anticipation that's based on your past experiences. It is something that has not actually happened – it is only an expectation. So the future also is nothing but some expectations, some electronic garbage in your mind. Your mind loves these two areas, and hates to be in the present. And for today, that is exactly your challenge.

Let's get one thing very clear – I am not trying to tell you to completely disconnect yourself from your past. Of course, you need to learn from your past. Similarly, you must plan the future – an unplanned future will never yield the results that we expect. However, please realise that most of us don't stop at that.

Dwelling on either the past or the future makes it a big burden on you. You are sure to get under this weight and experience problems. Too much of dwelling on the past results in guilt – and too much of future orientation is a source of worry. Both of these are extremely dangerous, for they will surely obstruct your view of the present.

The best strategy to avoid these two ghosts is to stay centered in the present. You need to be with what is happening right now. This will come with long and sustained practice, once you start it. Not that the mind will automatically come to the present, but you'll have to gently bring it here. The moment you become aware of your mind that's diverted, gently bring it back to the present, without any force.

In this way, you will be able to gradually stay in the present.

Truly, a life focussed in the present moment is a real life. Live this type of a life…. From today onwards.

IN PRACTICE

1. Get up from your bed as soon as you are awake. The time that you spend in lazing on the bed leads to wastage of unnecessary mental energy, which results in a tired mind throughout the day. Again, at night you must go to bed only when you feel asleep. Lying on the bed and thinking wildly is the most unproductive habit. Sleep with the surrender of all your worries to God.

2. Make a commitment to yourself at the beginning of every day to be in the present as much as possible. Decide not to speak to anyone of any past event. Soon this will become a habit and your life will no longer be a burden of the past or a fear of the future.

3. To ensure that you don't dwell in the past, heal it. Your present is affected to a great extent by your past. Forgive yourself for all your mistakes. Remember whatever you did at any given moment in the past, it was the best way you could do it. So don't regret it.

"There is no hope in the future where there is no power in the present." ◆ ◆

24. Just for Today I Will Listen More Than I Speak

If there is one thing that applies to almost all people without exception, it is their desire to be heard. More than a helping hand or a piece of mind, what people do need is an attentive ear. To listen to their problems, worries and all that they have to say. So just for today, you have to become a listener.

Swami Chinmayananda has said something really interesting about this. He says that God has given you many clues when he has made this body – and one such clue relates to this topic as well. Do you know why you have two ears, but only one mouth? You guessed it, if you've thought that you must listen twice about what you speak.

Most of us are interested in ourselves. It is something that applies to everyone. Consequently, people go on talking about themselves all the time. If a conversation is going in some general direction, they will make every attempt to include themselves in the topic. Ask them to write a letter to someone, and you'll notice the high number of 'I's. But this is perfectly normal, it's human nature.

A really magical transformation comes, though, when you begin to put others first. When you start to do that, you will see how well people react to you – it's just like treating others as you'd like to be treated. People need to be heard – and you can give them that through this practice.

One of my best friends, Hemang Panchmatia, is a living example of this. As I gained my reputation as a great speaker, he was gaining increasing acceptance as a great conversationalist. However much I tried, people would always open up to him much more than me. I couldn't hold myself and had to ask him the secret of this. What he told me was astonishing and to this date, remains one of the most interesting insights in my life.

Hemang said that being a great conversationalist was all about one secret – being a great listener. Hemang always used to listen more than speak, and that's what made him the loveable friend of everyone around. Initially, I couldn't believe that it could be as simple as that, but gradually, as I applied that policy, I realised how powerful it can be. Indeed, what he said was true.

When you become a good listener, it's not all about just talking less. Listening is something that has to be learnt. For even if you don't talk more and listen, people will still open up more to some people. The simple reason for this is the fact that your body language betrays you if you're not interested in listening fully; your body will send clues that the other person will pick up. It's something like vibes – the feeling that you get with the other person.

When you listen, you have to be very responsive. If your mind is wandering all around the world, how will you ever be able to focus on the person opposite you? So give all your attention to the other person. We've already talked about treating every person you meet as the most important person in the world.

Listening effectively starts with an intention to get the state of the mind of the communicator – it is your goal to grasp fully what the other person is trying to say. Feedback is equally important – it involves communicating through verbal/non-verbal clues that you are getting the message.

There are a few very irritating things you can do to spoil a conversation. Among them, the most common that I have observed (it was my habit too!) was to complete sentences for others. It is a typical situation where the receiver actually tries to complete sentences for the sender. It becomes a guessing game between the two – as a result the communication becomes a competition!

Another wrong thing is to interrupt when something interesting is going on. Interrupting a person is a surest way to spoil the communication. You will see that the best of listeners don't ever interrupt, but listen patiently. They wait for the person to complete, and then go on to start what they were saying. This is not easy, especially if this is a habit. It took me a long time to change it too. But with sustained practice and conscious effort, what is impossible?

Thus, just for today, you'll spend time listening. It is a beautiful way to absorb knowledge from others. And remember, to become a great speaker you need to have been a great listener at some time or the other. Let people observe the change for themselves.

IN PRACTICE

1. Just for today, consciously spend time listening to a friend. During this time you'll practice all the strategies that you've learnt.
2. Ask for feedback – how well you did as a listener – and you will be able to improve on things.
3. While communicating, try to listen to the unsaid also. Sometimes, people just want to be heard or are asking for attention. Knowing the true purpose of the communication will put you in a position to gain from it.
4. If today you were paid 1 rupee for every word you heard, and 2 rupees for every word you spoke, what would your balance be?

Date	Balance
14/2/02	Very Positive
15/2/02	Neutral

Fill this up till you generate a "Very Positive" comment for one whole week!

◆ ◆

25. Just for Today I Will be Non-Judgemental

"That was an awful movie I saw yesterday!"

"Don't ever talk to him – he is the most unfriendly person I've ever seen."

"Trust no women – they are all the same."

If you observe our daily conversations, you'll see that there is one thing that is common – as humans we constantly have a tendency to judge. We always label things, and constantly keep giving decisions as to whether they are good or bad or ugly.

It's almost as if you are the judge in a court and as every person and event comes, you pronounce your judgement on the person. You are the ultimate authority, and once a person gets a tag, he will have that forever. So if a person was labeled unkind he'll be that way for most of the time you know him, or at least till the time you know him better.

What are your judgement tags based upon? On the first impressions of the people in most cases – the way people appear or what you've heard of them. That's common with all of us. As the saying goes, "Don't judge a book by its cover." But when you judge, you are doing exactly that. You are deciding things on the basis of first impressions. Most of it is not likely to be true, but leads you to prejudice.

On the other hand, this must also act as a pointer to you – recognise the fact that others judge you constantly, and you must remember that most often your first impression on people will be a lasting one. Remember that consciously, when you meet new people. All humans are creatures that judge. Use this knowledge to your benefit.

What happens when you judge? Every time you pass judgement on something, you're colouring your perception of it. You're blocking any further improvement of the person's image in your mind. Most probably, you will also keep that opinion in mind when dealing with the person.

Apart from putting your mind into a prejudiced mode, there is one more thing that judging does – starting an excessively fast internal dialogue.

You've seen that most of the times the whole challenge of a person like you is to control the thoughts that come into your mind. All your practices are ultimately geared towards that only. The ultimate goal of all spiritual pursuit can be said to be mind control.

But this judging will lead you further away from this – it will make your mind noisy and full of chatter. It will also make the thoughts coming to your mind much faster – thereby causing you to lose focus. More thoughts will also mean a tired mind and weak intentions.

You may say this practice is almost impossible – well, I do agree that this is one of the most challenging JFTs of this book. But fret not, for with practice you will be able to reach the golden throne of non-judgement.

Every time you judge,
You will bear a grudge.

A prayer in the book *A Course in Miracles* states: "Just for today, I will judge nothing that occurs." This means that you will be non-judgemental all day. If you catch yourself passing some judgement or labelling, just become aware of it and stop. Tell yourself mentally "Stop". The mind will respond instantly, but soon may get back to its old ways. Realise that the mind is like a child and has to be handled with patience.

If you can't do this for a whole day, start your practice with hours, and then finally increase. For example, tell yourself that you'll not judge for the next one or two hours. As you start doing that successfully, go for extended periods of non-judgement.

So from today, a very challenging practice starts. And that is – not to judge.

IN PRACTICE

1. Start by deciding the time that you're going to remain non-judgemental.
2. Also make a list of the type of judgements you think you've passed, till date.
3. Now, record whether you could stick to your non-judgemental behaviour or not. Be warned, though, this is one of the most challenging but rewarding principles of this book.

Date	Passed Judgement(s) About

Exercise

We need to develop the innocence of a child when we look at things around us – the same wonder and curiosity, the same sweet and trusting attitude.

Pick up any object around you.

Now look at it as if you did not know it – just describe it as if it was not known to you at all, neither the qualities nor the uses.

This exercise will give you some insight into learning to be non-judgemental.

♦ ♦

26. Just for Today I Will Not Argue at All

"It is this way I say!"

"No way! It can never be – it has to be this way!"

I don't know the issue of this particular conversation. I don't know the people who are having it. Neither do I know what the outcome of this will be. But yes, I do know a few things when I realise that this is an argument.

I understand that there are two people here who have closed their ears. That there are two people who want to defend their egos – two people who can't listen to the other person. I know that more than the issue the fight is over who is right. And that the underlying assumption to this, of course, is that only one person can be correct at one point of time.

To me, an argument is the best way to make enemies. The truth about an argument is that it seldom ends with one person convincing the other. More often it ends in a fight. It ends in hurt. It ends in resentment. No one ever has been convinced through a full-fledged argument – in fact, once people take a stand in an argument they are more likely to stick to it. They will, in all probability, make sure that even if they are convinced, they do not admit it.

An argument is rightly called a double-edged sword. On one side, it hurts the person on whom it is used. So when you argue with someone, the other person is most likely to feel sad – especially the way you feel after you lose an argument. Spiritually, people who lose the argument lose their energy and feel disempowered.

On the other hand, an argument also hurts the other person concerned – which is you. What do you gain out of it? Nothing but some satisfaction that you have convinced the other person – if you actually have! But what's the use of that, especially when you realise that this is achieved at somebody else's cost – by causing hurt and resentment to others.

Somehow, I feel we have an intrinsic need of approval. There is a feeling that what you feel is right must be reciprocated – i.e. everyone must feel so. At the same time each one of us also knows that we are unique, and that it is almost impossible for everyone to agree on something, simply because each one of us feels so differently.

Look at the world – and humanity as a whole. We have not even been able to agree on the same God! We fight wars because we don't accept our differences. But if there is one thing that you need to learn from this, it is that other opinions will always exist, whatever you do.

It all starts with a decision from your end to not argue at all – to be defenceless. Your point of view is not always attacked, but more often than not, you interpret it as one. As soon as someone puts forth a view that is different from yours, you take it as an attack on yourself. Realise that one of the fundamental rights you have is to stick to your viewpoint.

When you argue, you spend a lot of useless energy. You create a lot of frustration in your own life, and reduce the speed of your spiritual evolution. There is a lot of scope to progress much beyond your limits – you can actually reach for more. Just avoid these distractions called arguments.

IN PRACTICE

1. Consciously watch for statements that provoke some sort of action or argument from you.
2. As soon as you are about to start an argument, use a delaying technique. A delaying technique is what creates a time gap between your thought and action. One of the best ones that I know of is to count to ten. The other is to mentally use the word "Stop".
3. Keep track of the times you actually went into an argument – you must count even the mildest discussions.

Resolution: I will be defenceless!

Date	Person	Cause

◆ ◆

27. Just for Today I Will Enjoy Little Things

Most of us have a pre-decided rule as to when we will be happy. You too must be having your own ideas about the same. Like when you complete the current course of education that you are pursuing, or when you earn a certain amount of money. It's only then that you will allow yourself to be happy. Till then you are doing something like delayed gratification – postponing your happiness.

This reminds me of a story of the legendary Mulla Nasruddin who's friend was returning from the market. He had just purchased a duck that they were going to cook for dinner. He looked really sad and tired in life. "What's wrong?" Mulla asked his friend.

"Everything, if you ask me. I'm looking for happiness but still haven't found it…."

"Oh, so you haven't found happiness as yet?" Mulla inquired.

As the friend was nodding slowly, Mulla Nasruddin suddenly snatched the duck from his friend and started running. Worried, the friend ran after him, desperate to get the duck back. A long chase followed, after which finally the friend caught up with Mulla and immediately snatched the duck back. He was relieved and happy that he had the duck back.

"Did you find it?" Mulla asked, smiling.

"What?"

"Happiness!" said Mulla.

The moment you understand this beautiful story, realisation will dawn on you. And that is that you don't need to wait to be happy or enjoy things. Life is filled to the brim with trifles that can make you really happy. Like success, happiness can't be a destination. It is a journey that you undertake. And the whole journey is filled with precious moments that give you true joy.

Most of us keep waiting for something big to happen that we lose sight of the smaller joys of life. And if you have the eye to appreciate, life is filled all along with such tidbits of joy – all so beautiful, if only you cared to enjoy them. Most of us are in search of that elusive big breakthrough before we would permit ourselves to be happy. My question is – why wait?

Ultimately, what happens when you reach the point you had waited for? You feel a moment of true joy – because for a moment your mind is calmed. You get a real glimpse of your inner self. But the moment you actually feel that, the next immediate thing to strike you is a major withdrawal symptom. You start feeling a sense of emptiness, because something that you had based your life upon all this time has suddenly happened. What next?

On the other hand, a life that's lived for the joy of living is an art. Every moment around you there are sights and events that can give you untold joy – pleasures that you'd never dream of. All you need do is discover that joy, which already resides in you.

Where do you look for trifles? Everywhere around! It could be the smile of a child that can make an entirely bad day perfectly all right. It could be a beautiful flower, or a sunset or a butterfly that you see. You can feel the joy of watching something so natural and perfect! It can be a talk with a friend or a joke that you hear. It can be the call of some exotic bird.

Such things have always been around you all the time. All you need do is stand up and look. You need to notice, and you'll see the grandeur. You'll see the beauty and joy that you'd been missing. Take your goal like a delicacy – bite by bite. And don't forget to enjoy each bite – the total will be more than what you'd ever achieve by eating the whole thing at once.

Remember, trifles make true happiness.

IN PRACTICE

1. Start by listing some happiness rules – when will you be happy? What has to happen in order for you to be happy?

_____
_____
_____

2. Now decide to look for small joys throughout the day, all around you. This decision itself will have far-reaching effects.
3. At the end of the day, make a list of events that you really felt happy about.

_____
_____
_____

◆◆

28. Just for Today I Will Learn One New Skill

I am a teacher and it is one vocation that's more like a vacation for me. I really love to teach others, and make a difference to their lives in the process. I love my students, and most of them find me a good teacher. But there is one very important thing that I know about being a good teacher – to be a good teacher, I need to be a great student. I can't teach what I have not learnt myself.

If you look at your own learning curve, you'll see that it almost stagnated beyond your teens. After that you hardly learnt anything consciously. The student within you has gone into a deep sleep. And this strategy is the one that will help you awaken that student within you.

The first question that probably comes up is why should someone actually learn? Many reasons can be given for that. The primary one is because learning is nothing but growth for your mind. The way a mind grows is through learning. As you learn new things, associations are formed in your mind, and your overall ability to understand and comprehend also increases.

Apart from that, not learning to me is a sign of arrogance. Too many of us are very satisfied with our initial success, and believe that that's what life is all about. We have a false notion that we are perfect, and that's what prevents us from learning. And not learning breeds ignorance. In this ignorance, you make mistakes, and from such mistakes comes fear. That's the whole cycle for you.

Now if you look at learning you'll see that life is nothing but a learning process. It's the way we are designed to evolve. Each one of us makes mistakes, but gets up and moves on. That's what makes humans so unique, and this is one of the skills modern computers are trying to incorporate as they attempt to build up artificial intelligence.

So just for today, you will become a learner. You will look at learning a new skill. Yes, not all skills can be learnt in a day. But at least a start can be made. If the skill is cooking, you can learn one recipe for today and make it yourself. If it's singing you can learn one more song to add to your collection. You can learn speed-reading or any other skill. It's your choice.

What skill you pick up will largely depend on things that you've always wanted to do. Try and think of things that you've always been interested in. There is no person on this planet who isn't interested in anything. There has to be some area of life where you will learn and grow.

The source that you learn from is also very important. It may sound very obvious, but if you learn from someone who's not so strong, you'll tend to pick up almost the same mistakes in your own skill. You have a choice. Always pick up a mentor – someone who has mastered a skill over a lifetime. There are also many books, audio-tapes or TV programmes that you can watch to master.

Remember that consistency in learning is the key. You don't want to end up as a jack of all trades and master of none, do you? It's things that you do consistently, not occasionally, that ultimately determine your destiny. So just make sure you develop yourself as you learn the skill. And who knows? We may have a master on our hands.

IN PRACTICE

1. Make a list of the skills that you've always wanted to master.

_____
_____
_____
_____
_____

2. Now pick up the skill and list parts of it – e.g. if it's cooking, you can split it up as the number of recipes that you could make.

_____
_____
_____

3. The final step of course is action – start the learning. Don't forget to record the experience in your journal.

◆◆

29. Just for Today I Will See Things from Somebody Else's Point of View

Perceptions count more than reality – one of the principles that I've learnt while working with so many different organisations. Each one of us has a different way of looking at things. For someone the glass may be half-full, while for someone else it may be half-empty! It's only the way you look at it. And each one of our ways is different.

Look at a snap of a crowd in a huge cricket stadium. From that distance, most of the people will seem almost the same. But that is not the truth, for as you zoom closer into the picture, you'll see the differences gradually emerge. Till in the end you discover that each one of us is extremely different from the others.

Why this difference? Because of many factors. For one, the genetic difference itself makes it virtually impossible to have someone genetically identical to you. You are unique – like everyone else! Then there are childhood influences – each one of us has had different experiences that have led to the development of certain attitudes. These attitudes will eventually decide how you interpret what happens to you. Finally these memories will form beliefs and references, creating the unique person that you are.

More often than not, we have a wrong belief that everyone else will think like us. If each one of us is so very unique, most of our thinking also will be. I remember one of my friends who said that he would only marry someone who had the same beliefs as him. He wanted someone of the same thoughts and faith – in short a clone. Biologically itself, the chances of finding someone identical is one in a trillion! And we are far away from that mark.

You must realise that everyone is different. In spirituality, awareness itself is a very powerful tool. It let's you bring something into focus. When you do this, you will automatically accept the fact that others are different. This is very similar to not arguing or remaining defenceless.

Seeing things from another's point of view is all about stepping into the other person's shoes. You'll see where it pinches. Not everyone has gone through the same things that you have. You might have seen more of life. You may have suffered much more pain. You have really seen the best and the worst of it.

Coincidentally, everyone else also thinks so too! So when you are into knowing a person, one of the greatest gifts that you can give is to see things from his point of view. Try to understand his angle of the story. Try to know why he is saying what he is, rather than trying to attack it.

It's basically all about reading between the lines – it's hearing what is not said. So I know when my mom is scolding me about something, she is concerned. Instead of feeling bad about her shout, I feel happy that there is someone who cares.... And that makes all the difference.

At this very moment I offer you two choices – two roads to choose from. One is the conventional way – on which you will remain absorbed and self-centered. On this way your viewpoint will be all about yourself – like most of the people you meet. The other is the road less travelled. It's a path where you dedicate your life to seeing things from the other point of view. It's a path where you practice and try to understand what the other person is saying. Choose the road less travelled, and it'll make all the difference.

I'm not telling you to change your views on any issue. Please don't misunderstand the point about looking at things from the other person's viewpoint. The aim is not to mould your thoughts to the other person's choice. That will make you one of the most gullible persons around! Neither is the intention to try and get the other person to see your stand on an issue.

The whole aim is that you must get a broader picture. When you've seen both sides of the coin, you've seen the whole of it. And that insight will make you far wiser than when you were sticking only to your viewpoint. Another wonderful thought – I've yet to come across a coin where both sides are the same.

People want to be heard, and respected. When you accept their viewpoint, they will become more responsive to you. They will be themselves, for you'll not be one who passes judgements and demands changes. In this unconditional acceptance you will bring out the beauty in them. Again, the aim is not that you stop suggesting positive changes to people. In fact, after accepting their stand, people will become more receptive to you. Having seen that you care, your suggestions will have more weight.

Isn't this a wonderful strategy? A simple way through which big changes can be brought about. I hope you'll look at this one from my point of view too!

IN PRACTICE

1. Just for today, you must be an aggressive observer. Constantly see what the other person is trying to say, for as much as 70% of your communication will be non-verbal. If you can do that, it will give you deeper insights about people.
2. Whenever you hear an idea contrary to yours keep an open mind – don't jump on it or criticise it. Let the idea seep in, it may be worth it.
3. Similarly, don't react when someone opposes you. Just for today, you must agree to disagree with such people!
4. Ask questions to people if you fully don't understand what they are trying to say. This is also a gentle way of guiding conversations away from the problem issues.
5. Read one publication that you disagree with – it can be a book or a newspaper. When you read such views, you will be able to see things from the other side and get a holistic perspective of the issue.

Observe the expansion of your viewpoint....

◆◆

30. Just for Today I Will Do the One Thing I had been Postponing

If you sit up right now and decide to make a list of things that you plan to do, you'll find a huge list. Try it right now. Think of the unread books. You may have some appointments with the doctor, or some phone calls to make. Others may have requested you to do some work that you have been postponing. Then there will be things that fit in the "I always wanted to" category. Do you know why the list is so long? Because you had been postponing them.

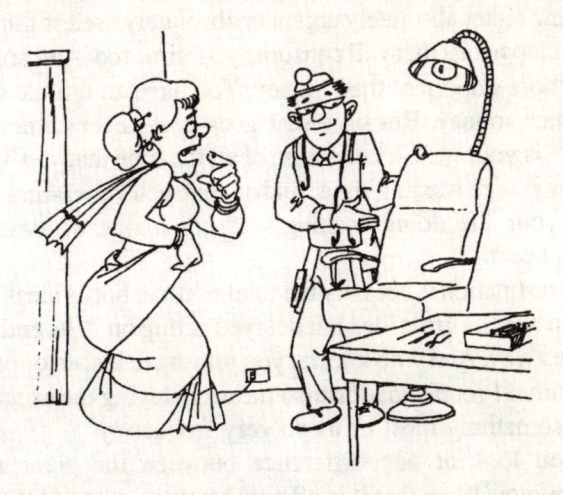

A sad but true part of being humans is that we seek gratification. The entire outlook that we have mainly focuses on the short term – you see if anything is enjoyable in the short term or not. All of us are almost driven by quick fixes. So when the time to visit the dentist comes, you postpone the check up. You have a party to go to that will not come again. The dentist is always there.

Then the next time some important work comes up. The dentist can wait. This continues for long, till your poor body gives you an action signal – a toothache! Now you have no choice but to rush to the "always there" dentist. But this will come in between some other task. We all live our lives in the fast lane.

You may have planned some work for the evening but your favourite movie is on the TV – how can you miss it? So you push the work for late. Then you may sit up late night and complete it, only to get a late start for the next day. What I'm trying to show you is that we constantly create the procrastination web – where we get entangled.

It's a fact of life that there are certain things that you have to do – like work, or self-care. If you miss that, you're in for some trouble. When there is time for things to be done, they are minor. But they grow in size as deadlines approach, till they seem like huge monsters that can't be killed. They overpower you, and you surrender. It's a typical example of the life that we live.

And in this type of an unplanned life, you will always spend time doing either absolutely urgent or absolutely useless things. You will develop habits that will consume your time too. And remember, time is more important than money. You have an infinite capacity to generate money. But time that goes past never comes back.

What is your life? A collection of all the time that you've spent. So when you're wasting time, realise that you're wasting a major part of your life doing nothing – if not major, at least a very important part.

Procrastination is not only the thief of time, but of ideas as well. If you've had the great idea but delayed acting on it, its enthusiasm will fade away. And who knows, you may have lost an opportunity of a lifetime! Procrastination also means delaying the execution of ideas – something most of us do very frequently.

If you look at one difference between the great and the mediocre, you'll see that it is all about how they spend their time. It's about how they have treated ideas. If research is to be believed, such ideas strike most people, most of the times. But a far lesser percentage of people actually act on them, which means that there are more failures than successes.

So just for today, you'll clear the backlog of things that you've wanted to do since a long time. An unfinished task is a big burden on the mind too. Much bigger than you think it is. When you leave something that's unfinished, it dwells in your mind. As kids we used to tell stories of souls who turned into ghosts and haunted people to fulfill their unrequited wishes! If your soul could be probed, would it attain salvation or turn into a ghost wanting to do so many things it had never done but always wanted to?

Things that you've not done will also haunt your mind. Many people complain of recurring thoughts. These are generally fears or unlived experiences. The secret to removing or dealing with both these types of thoughts is taking action. It is said that feel the fear and do it anyway. If it's an unlived experience, something that you wanted to do, just do it!

Psychology is finding out deeper connections between your thoughts and your body. Every thought produces a chemical reaction in your body. And you'll see that the procrastinators' mind will generally be occupied with more agitation and thoughts about finishing things.

Where does this end? The answer is self-discipline. It's in maintaining a long-term perspective of things – you need to look at an action before you do it and ask yourself whether there is any long-term gain involved in this. Are you investing in yourself?

Treat time like money – be very conscious of where it is spent. If this spending is not in your control right now, take action and get it into your control. If you don't the price to be paid for it could be really heavy.

IN PRACTICE

1. First make a list of things that you've been postponing.

_____
_____

2. Also list out things that fall in the always-want-to-do category.

_____
_____

3. Attach deadlines to them – when you will accomplish them.
4. At the start of the day, or preferably on the previous day, just make a list of the things that you want to do the next day – keep looking at it and you'll see that it happens!
5. Finally, don't give in to instant gratification. Reward yourself every time you do something that you've been postponing. Soon you'll become a master of the time that you spend, and do that at will.

◆◆

31. Just for Today I Will Take Positive Feedback

As this book comes to a close, I present you the most profound of the learning that I've ever received. If there is one single principle that has worked all my life, it is this one. And so, before you close this book, take with yourself this wisdom of ages that I have to share...

Sounds too much for a simple strategy like this one? Don't jump to conclusions so soon! If there is one Just for Today that you decide to devote yourself completely to, let it be this one. If there is one that you can share with friends, and apply all your life, it's taking positive feedback.

Feedback is the breakfast of champions. Failures come to all of us – the people who are richest in our society have lost the most money too. The best speakers have tackled stage fear too. Even the best of your sports persons were raw at some point of time or the other. The essence is feedback. That's the difference between the ordinary and the extraordinary – so small yet so profound.

Throughout this book we've shared strategies to build a happier and better life. If you've tried all of them, congratulations! You form a part of the less than 10% people who actually go on to read the entire book and apply it. Not all of these techniques may have worked. Maybe, not even one worked. What's wrong?

If you look at Just for Today, it's nothing more than a compilation of common wisdom. It's things that we forget so easily. When you take the opinions of others, you are actually also sending out a message to them that says you care.

Being the football of others' opinions is not what I'm suggesting – you need to be very careful when you take feedback. Only do that from people who really care about you – there is a very thin line between feedback and criticism. Don't be so soft that the criticism will hurt you – you must be open to all that comes in, but filter everything on the screen of truth.

Humans are never perfect, and we were never meant to be – but it can always be a goal that you want to reach someday. Perfection can never be completely attained, because life is a constant process of improvement. Keep reinventing yourself and you will never ever be behind.

Life is either a daring adventure or nothing.

–Helen Keller

Make your life an adventure – go and reach for all that you desire. But remember that just as Rome was not built in a day, the changes also will come very slowly. V-e-r-y s-l-o-w-l-y. You will have to be patient. And when they do come, you'll be surprised at the paradigm shift that has happened in your life.

The reason why the opinions of others are so important is that we have a completely different view of ourselves – our strengths and weaknesses. The other view is that seen by the outside world. Now both are important, but there is a subtle difference in the two – while one is very easy to see mistakes from, the other remains a mystery. So feedback is the key.

Keep improving all the time, but start today. Just for today, make a new start!

IN PRACTICE

Make a feedback log where you take positive as well as negative feedback from the people who are closest to you. If they are uncomfortable saying it to you, let them write it to you in the form of a letter.

Person	Feedback

Keep doing this periodically and take action on the feedback you receive **if, and only if, you think it is appropriate.** No one in this world can judge this better than you.

◆◆

CAN is the world of POWER

—*Barendra Kumar*

A confidence building approach for Millions of Young Minds

A Life-making, Powerful, Inspirational Plan and Work Book

You CAN Have More of You
You CAN Build a Better You
You CAN Yield a Greater You

"I liked you can yield a greater you.... My best wishes..."
—*Dr. A.P.J. Abdul Kalam*

Inspiration and motivation, undoubtedly increases effectiveness and efficiency. Thus, it is far more essential for the young minds of the nation than anybody else to help them DREAM BIG, AIM HIGH for improvements, innovations and inventions, which can be possible by strong positive thought, acquisition of creative/inventive ideas and its execution according to strategic plan of action for the peace, progress and prosperity of self and society.

CAN is... POWER not only advocates the same, but also covers all aspects of personal growth —spiritual, emotional, physical, mental, and inspires to make a successful career to build a meaningful life. Needless to say, it is equally useful for average to excelling students, as well as their custodians/well-wishers.

This book, for self-analysis, improvement and success, with hundreds of inspirational quotes and hints of stories of different event makers, from different countries — past and present — to expand the databank, will surely induce success thinking for better personal and national living.

Demy Size • Pages: 278
Price: Rs. 150/- • Postage: Rs. 20/-

Secrets of HAPPINESS

—Tanushree Podder

We must look inwards as happiness is within us, like salt in the ocean

Happiness is a feeling of joy and gratitude that is more often than not fleeting. There are no magic mantras that will impart joy and happiness when recited continuously. It is only by developing a positive and cheerful attitude towards life that one can be happy. For peace of mind and contentment, we need to look inwards rather than outwards. We need to find peace within ourselves because it is not available through other means – no matter what price one is willing to pay. The book delineates ways and means to ensure happiness in every walk of life.

But the purpose of this book stretches beyond the visible endeavour of outlining codes of happiness. It also encompasses the need to bring in a little light in our otherwise gloomy lives. Many of the inspirational stories in this book will succeed in doing just that.

Demy Size • Pages: 192
Price: Rs. 96/- • Postage: Rs. 15/-

What's your Emotional I.Q.

—*Aparna Chattopadhyay*

Over 600 Psychological Quizzes

Assess your weaknesses and strengths in your emotions & feelings and groom fuller personality.

This fascinating book authored by Dr. Aparna Chattopadhyay, offers you a new vision of self-awareness which would enable you to assess your feelings, capabilities and aptitudes. As you develop self-awareness, you will not only be able to identify the emotional patterns in your life and will manage them well, but will also be able to activate all-round personality development.

It will help you lead life more powerfully than before through a wide range of Psychological Quizzes.

This book enables you to:

- Generate fresh enthusiasm and ambition in your life.
- Live more happily and effectively.
- Build self-confidence and develop inner peace.
- Enjoy better interpersonal relationships.
- Rid yourself of unwanted negative emotions.
- Protect your self from stress.
- Cultivate positive thinking.
- Trigger creativity.
- Enjoy better mental and physical health.
- Cultivate spiritual awareness.

Demy Size • Pages: 176
Price: Rs. 80/- • Postage: Rs. 10/-

Winning Résumé

—*Jayant Neogy*

How to write an impressive Curriculum Vitae (CV) that guarantees you an interview call ...And the rest is achievable, undoubtedly.

Your résumé is your first introduction to the employer who has never seen you before. You need to give it the best shot to make the first winning move. The book 'Winning Résumé' fulfils this long-felt need for a contemporary guide on résumé writing that is in line with the expectations of global employers in this information technology driven age. The book breaks away from the traditional world of sequential cataloguing of degrees and job histories. Instead, it provides candidates seeking new jobs or job changes with contemporary techniques to fulfil a difficult task, to produce polished, subtle and refined advertisement-copy about their own selves.

This book is the result of an extensive research, practical experience and deep insight. There are practical guidelines for crafting a winning résumé that will stand out amongst a thousand others. Key points are highlighted throughout the book by using bold text on the left side of paragraphs; useful 'tips' are identified by figures of a wise owl. To point out errors and grave mistakes in résumés 'traps' are identified by figures of skull and crossbones. After going through the book the readers will get a thorough understanding of the changes in philosophy and techniques that have revolutionized presentation of curriculum vitae. It is a sure-shot for success in one's pursuit of an illustrious career.

Demy Size • Pages: 136
Price: Rs. 80/- • Postage: Rs. 15/-

Success Through POSITIVE THINKING

—*S.P. Sharma*

Is half full better or half empty?
* Choose right
* Think better
* Live well

Present-day life has become too complex and complicated. There is a scramble for more and more. Money, power and wealth have become symbols of success and happiness. A confused sense of affairs and lopsided values, that's leading to a lot of tension and distress.

Now **Success Through Positive Thinking** shows you the way out. Advocating a change of attitude through moderation, acceptance of things as they are, and inculcating of moral values. The result? A positive personality free of negative elements like anxiety, stress, greed, envy and jealousy!

An Overview

Success Through Positive Thinking shows you the right path to real happiness through:
❖ A proper perspective on life
❖ Meditations and prayers
❖ Importance of work
❖ Handling of criticism and slander
❖ Knowing the difference between right and wrong, real and unreal
❖ Proper channelizing of sexual and physical energy.

Demy Size • Pages: 180
Price: Rs. 80/- • Postage: Rs. 15/-

Understanding Emotional I.Q.

—*Dr. Jyotsna Codaty*

The Mantra for Human Relationship

According to new researchers, an emotionally strong person is better adjusted to his work environments and more capable of handling social and personal relationship. Thus he is in a better position to lead a more successful, wholesome and fulfilling life.

Although everyone has a certain ingrained emotional personality, there is always scope for improvements. In this well-researched volume, Dr. Jyotsna Codaty, a medical practitioner and motivator, shows how to improve one's emotional personality with clear-cut examples of different types of behavioural patterns, with findings of leading psychoanalysts like Meslow and Hans Selye. Citing examples of model personality like Mahatma Gandhi, she analyses basic emotions—e.g. anger, love, fear, phobia or sadness with sound tips on how to manage their extreme forms.

This book is amply illustrated with examples and test charts in the Indian contexts and sensibly designed to strengthen your emotional aptitude to achieve perfection in your life!

- ❖ Keep your focus sharp to gain an unshakable confidence.
- ❖ Set your motivation high.
- ❖ Master the key attitudes and discover greater levels of success in your life!

Demy size, Pages: 128
Price: Rs. 68/- • Postage: Rs. 15/-

Explore Your Hidden Talents

—*Dr. Aparna Chattopadhyay*

Over 40 self-analysis modules to help you achieve excellence in your career.

With the dawn of the new millennium, the average workplace is becoming more challenging than ever. A better insight into the dynamics of achieving success in one's job and business is the need of the hour. Success when viewed with a positive mental attitude, is a process. It is a journey - not the destination. Explore your own road to success by analyzing, recognizing, visualizing and mobilizing processes. Success is the process of managing your greatest asset— You.

This impressive self-help book authored by Dr. Aparna Chattopadhyay gives you new ways of energising your hidden qualities, potentials and possibilities of success in your business and career arenas to:

- Harness creativity & enthusiasm to work more productively and successfully.
- Identify your leadership strengths.
- Develop skills of management.
- Dream your way to reality.
- Pack the power of positive thinking into your work life.
- Learn the psycho-tricks of the trade.
- Revitalize and sterilize your attitude against all odds.
- Become a team player and strengthen cooperation among associates.
- Say "Hello" to success.

Demy Size • Pages: 174
Price: Rs. 120/- • Postage: Rs. 15/-

The Complete Guide to MEMORY MASTERY

—Harry Lorayne

ORGANISING & DEVELOPING THE POWER OF YOUR MIND

The memory is always present; ready and anxious to help if only we would ask it to do so more often. —Roger Broille

The more intelligible a thing is, the more easily it is retained in the memory, and contrariwise, the less intelligible it is, the more easily we forget it. —Benedict Spinoza

Thinking is the hardest work there is, which is the probable reason why so few engage in it. —Henry Ford

Don't thou love life! Then do not squander time, for that is the stuff life is made of. —Benjamin Franklin

Here, in one volume, you will learn his unique proven techniques to:

- Increase your powers of memory and concentration.
- Strengthen good habits and discard bad ones.
- Improve your powers of observation.
- Deliver a speech without fear.
- Become more organised and time-efficient.

Big Size • Pages: 312
Price: Rs. 160/- • Postage: Rs. 20/-

Youngster's Guide for Personality Development

—*S.P. Sharma*

A book for the young men and women, specially students, with Indian precepts and culture

This book seeks to motivate young men and women, particularly students, to make conscious and continuous effort to build character and develop personality. With deep insight, the author has provided valuable guidelines and practical steps on matters of special interest to students. Further, he has given them the benefit of experience, his own as well as those of eminent persons.

Considering the significant role of teachers and parents and their responsibility in moulding young minds, it is hoped that this book will be welcomed by them too.

Demy size, Pages: 120
Price: Rs. 80/- • Postage: Rs. 15/-

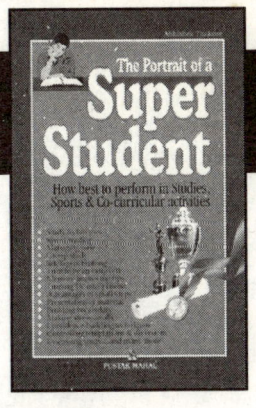

The Portrait of a Super Student

—*Abhishek Thakore*

How best to perform in Studies, Sports & Co-curricular activities

Success today depends a lot on one's academic achievements. And to excel in studies, you don't have to be just an intelligent or brilliant student—but also one who knows how to manage studies and time. In fact even a mediocre or a below-average student can perform exceedingly well by following a scientific system.

The Portrait of a Super Student now brings you an innovative system specifically designed for super achievement. From simple, practical and time-tested tips on how to manage time, controlling temptation, scheduling time and work, relaxing techniques to diet control, speed reading, building vocabulary, improving presentation, discussing studies it goes on to guide how to make stress an ally, make a friend out of your TV and delaying gratification, besides others. And above all, to make it reader-friendly the book is divided into easy-to-read small chapters—with a practice section after every chapter.

Demy Size • Pages: 144
Price: Rs. 80/- • Postage: Rs. 15/-